WILLIAM J. ROTHWELL, EDITOR

Contributing Authors:
Michele Brock
Peter J. Dean
Marc J. Rosenberg
Ethan S. Sanders

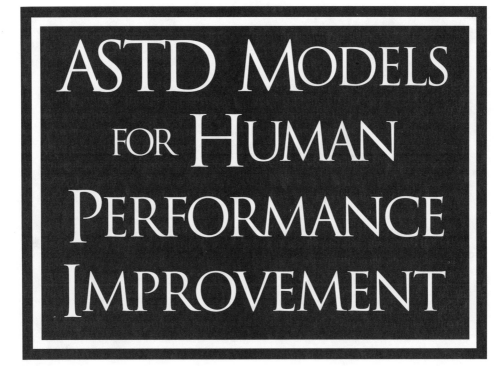

ASTD MODELS FOR HUMAN PERFORMANCE IMPROVEMENT

ROLES, COMPETENCIES, AND OUTPUTS

SECOND EDITION

ASTD

Ordering Information: Books published by the American Society for Training and Development can be ordered by calling 703.683.8100.

1640 King Street
Box 1443
Alexandria, VA 22313-2043
PH 703.683.8100, FX 703.683.8103
www.astd.org

Library of Congress Catalog Card Number: 99-73433

ISBN: 1-56286-126-3

◢ TABLE OF CONTENTS

◢ LIST OF FIGURES AND TABLES

Page

FOREWORD

In recent years organizations have been struggling to improve human performance and productivity, to address the issues associated with flexible or contingent workforces and reengineered workplaces, and to demonstrate return on human resource investments. Human resource development practitioners—like most managers and employees in today's fast-paced organizations—face these challenges as well. Gone are the days when HRD practitioners immediately assumed that training was the magic cure for all performance ills. Gone, too, are the days when the word *training* meant only classroom experiences offered at work. Today's HRD practitioners, managers, and employees must be aware of interventions other than training that support human performance improvement and learning. For these reasons, it is necessary to identify the roles, competencies, and expected outputs of those who do human performance improvement work.

This volume, published by the American Society for Training and Development, serves as a handbook, guide, and tool for those involved in reinventing today's workforce to make it more productive. It also serves to enhance novices' and practitioners' understanding of ways to improve human performance at work. HRD managers and practitioners can use this publication to help address the challenges associated with restructuring their training functions in order to incorporate human performance improvement concepts and techniques. Line managers and employees also will find *ASTD Models for Human Performance Improvement* useful as they assume key roles in enhancing the performance of their organizations while striving to meet their customers' escalating demands.

ASTD Models for Human Performance Improvement directs attention to the roles, competencies, outputs, ethical issues, future forces, and other issues affecting those involved in improving human performance.

Human performance improvement requires HRD practitioners, line managers, and others to

◆ identify past, present, or possible future performance gaps
◆ consider possible interventions to close performance gaps
◆ identify appropriate and optimal interventions
◆ evaluate how well interventions are closing human performance gaps and realizing human performance improvement potential.

As individuals engage in human performance improvement work, they are accountable for what they do. As a result, they must also demonstrate returns on investments in human performance improvement interventions.

I wish to acknowledge and express my appreciation to the principal author, William Rothwell, and to contributing authors Marc Rosenberg and Peter Dean. I also would like to thank the volunteer members of ASTD's Expert Panel for their efforts and support.

Many outstanding staff members also participated in the development of *ASTD Models for Human Performance Improvement*. From ASTD, Michele Brock served as project manager and a contributing author; Paul Elliott, Patricia Galagan, Greta Kotler, Nancy Olson, Mary Samsa, Ed Schroer, and Mark Van Buren provided ongoing advisory assistance; Theresa Minton-Eversole served as project editor; and Susan Wantland and Callie Norton served as directors of editorial and production services.

At this critical time for the profession, as we embark on new challenges that require new competencies, I fully expect this publication to be a significant contribution to the field research that addresses how to demonstrate return on investment for human performance improvement.

Curtis Plott

Curtis E. Plott
President Emeritus
American Society for Training & Development

The American Society for Training and Development has sponsored three ground breaking competency studies to date. The first was Pinto's and Walker's *Study of Professional Training and Development Roles and Competencies* (1978). The second was McLagan's and McCullough's *Models for Excellence* (1983). The third and most recent study was McLagan's *Models for HRD Practice* (1989), which served to fulfill the following purposes:

◆ Summarize 11 roles of HRD professionals, including that of researcher, marketer, organization change agent, needs analyst, program designer, HRD materials developer, instructor/facilitator, individual career development advisor, administrator, evaluator, and HRD manager.

◆ Identify and define 35 HRD competencies.

◆ Describe 74 outputs of HRD work.

◆ Identify quality requirements for each HRD output.

◆ Define human resource development as "the integrated use of training and development, organization development, and career development to improve individual, group, and organizational effectiveness," (McLagan, 1989, p.7).

◆ Position HRD within the larger human resources field through a Human Resource Wheel that encompasses the following: training and development, organization development, career development, organization/job design, human resource planning, performance management systems, selection and staffing, compensation and benefits, employee assistance, union/labor relations, and HR research and information systems.

◆ List 13 future forces affecting HRD: (1) increased pressure and capacity to measure workforce productivity, performance, cost-effectiveness, and efficiency; (2) increased pressure to demonstrate the value, impact, quality, and practicality of HRD services; (3) accelerated rate of change and more uncertain business environment; (4) increased emphasis on customer service and expectation of quality products and services from the workforce; (5) increased sophistication and variety of tools, technologies, methods, theories, and choices in HRD; (6) increased diversity (demographics, values, experience) at all levels of the workforce; (7) increased expectations for higher levels of judgment and flexibility in worker contribution (specifically, for creativity, risk taking, adaptation to change, and teamwork); (8) increased use of systems approaches that integrate HRD systems and technology in the workplace; (9) business strategies that concentrate more human resources and require strategic HRD actions;

(10) changed emphasis in organizations from loyalty to merit, accountability, performance, and relevant skills; (11) globalization of business; increased and expanded international markets, joint ventures, overseas ownerships, and competition; (12) increased need for commitment, meaningful work, and participation on the job by a larger proportion of the workforce; and (13) increased use of flatter, more flexible organization designs; smaller, self-contained work groups; and reduced staff (McLagan, 1989, pp. 13-14).

◆ Identify key ethical issues affecting HRD work, including maintaining appropriate confidentiality; saying "no" to inappropriate requests; showing respect for copyrights, sources, and intellectual property; ensuring truth in claims, data, and recommendations; balancing organizational and individual needs and interests; ensuring customer and user involvement, participation, and ownership; avoiding conflicts of interest; managing personal biases; showing respect for, interest in, and representation of individual and population differences; making the intervention appropriate to the customer's or user's needs; being sensitive to the direct and indirect effects of intervention and acting to address negative consequences; pricing or costing products or services fairly; and using power appropriately (McLagan, 1989, pp. 40-41).

Published in four volumes, *Models for HRD Practice* ambitiously builds on *Models for Excellence* and helps to explain the HRD practitioner's role in career and organization development. The first volume contains technical research results. The second volume, written for managers, provides instructions, tools, and guidelines to encourage mentoring consistent with the models. The third volume, written for HRD practitioners, contains worksheets to encourage self-development in line with the models. The fourth volume, which contains the models themselves, is a user's guide to the research results that summarize how the models may be used. A separately published but related fifth book entitled *The Academic Guide* (Nancy M. Dixon and Jim Henkelman, 1991) describes how to apply *Models for HRD Practice* to academic degree programs in HRD.

Many HRD practitioners have used the 1989 study. Accordingly, it has become apparent that efforts to improve human performance are evolving to encompass broader applications than training, organization, and career development. Managers increasingly demand accountability for results rather than request activities such as training. There is also a strong reliance on such emerging instructional technologies as distance education and electronic performance support systems. Instructional methods also include classroom or on-the-job training. Those involved in performance improvement are placing greater importance on managerial, supervisory, and worker involvement in planned learning experiences or human performance improvement change efforts (called interventions). And finally, there is an increased focus on real-time, just-in-time human performance improvement interventions, rather than efforts requiring long time spans for analysis, design, development, implementation, and evaluation.

The purpose of this book is comparable to the *Models* volume in *Models for HRD Practice*. It summarizes the results of this exploratory research to identify new roles, competencies, and outputs of people who do *human performance improvement* (HPI) work, and it helps readers understand what those results mean. It also provides practical guidance for line managers, HRD practitioners, and others who wish to enact the roles, build the competencies, and demonstrate the outputs associated with HPI work.

The book is divided into 9 sections, plus a glossary and reference list. Section 1 describes the methodology used to conduct the study and defines the term human performance improvement. Section 2 describes the foundation upon which HPI work is being built.

Human performance improvement is affected by trends, or future forces, and by changing conditions in organizational environments. These are described in Section 3 and serve as the backdrop against which human performance improvement roles are enacted, competencies are demonstrated, and outputs are achieved.

Section 4 introduces the human performance improvement process model, which is the basis for much of this study.

Section 5 lists the roles linked to the HPI process models, the competencies linked to the roles, and the outputs linked to the competencies. This section also includes an explanation of how to develop quality requirements for HPI work.

Section 6 describes key ethical issues associated with HPI work. These issues do not represent an exhaustive list, but are intended to serve as guidelines for those performing such work. Section 7 suggests audiences and uses for the book, and Section 8 summarizes the study and emphasizes its importance.

Section 9 provides tools that readers can use to apply the results of this study to their particular situations. Specifically, it provides the means to develop personal profiles that identify what HPI work they presently are doing, what HPI work they believe they should be doing, and what HPI work they should do in the future. The profiles of individuals undertaking human performance improvement work will vary, of course. These profiles will depend on organizational and stakeholder needs. This section also provides

◆ a questionnaire that individuals can use to solicit feedback from others about their competency levels
◆ a list of resources that can help individuals build the competencies associated with human performance improvement work
◆ a form that can be used to establish an individual development plan
◆ a worksheet that can be used to track trends and prepare for the future
◆ a worksheet that can be used to address possible ethical dilemmas faced during human performance improvement work.

Human performance improvement can be applied in many ways and by many people. This book does not attempt to present a job description for those performing HPI work. That would be too restrictive, considering the broad range of corporate cultures within which human performance improvement approaches can be used and the broad range of human performance improvement strategies that can be applied. The roles, competencies, and outputs are intended to provide guidance for aspiring, or experienced, HRD practitioners and others who are applying the principles of human performance improvement.

◢ ACKNOWLEDGMENTS

ASTD Models for Human Performance Improvement is based on an exploratory study conducted in 1995-1996. A panel of experts was created, based on their experience and contribution to the HRD profession, to review the elements of human performance improvement.

ASTD Expert Panel on Human Performance Improvement, 1995–1996

Mary L. Broad, *Ed.D.*
Principal Consultant
Performance Excellence
Chevy Chase, Maryland

Michele Brock
Project Manager, Market Development and
    Requirements Planning
American Society for Training and Development
Alexandria, Virginia

William Coscarelli, *Ph.D.*
Professor, Curriculum and Instruction
Southern Illinois University
Carbondale, Illinois
    and
Director, World Wide Test Development Center
Hewlett-Packard
Carbondale, Illinois

Peter J. Dean, *Ph.D.*
Associate Professor and Department Head
Department of Human Resource Development
College of Human Ecology
University of Tennessee
Knoxville, Tennessee

Paul Elliott, *Ph.D.*
Executive-in-Residence
American Society for Training and Development
Alexandria, Virginia
    and
President
Human Performance Technologies
Annapolis, Maryland

Patricia Galagan
Editor
Training & Development magazine
American Society for Training and Development
Alexandria, Virginia

Greta Kotler
Director, Market Development and
    Requirements Planning
American Society for Training and Development
Alexandria, Virginia

Nancy Kuhn
Vice-President, Education and Training
American Red Cross
Washington, D.C.

Danny G. Langdon
President
Performance International
Santa Monica, California

Ursula Lohmann, *Ph.D.*
Dean of Academics, Army Management Staff College
Department of the Army
Fort Belvoir, Virginia

Nancy Olson
Vice-President, Publications
American Society for Training and Development
Alexandria, Virginia

James C. Robinson
Chairman
Partners in Change, Inc.
Pittsburgh, Pennsylvania

Marc J. Rosenberg, *Ph.D.*
District Manager, Learning Strategy
AT&T
Somerset, New Jersey

William J. Rothwell, *Ph.D.*
Associate Professor, Human Resource Development
Department of Adult Education, Instructional Systems,
    and Workforce Education and Development
Pennsylvania State University
University Park, Pennsylvania

Mary Samsa
Manager, Forum Development
American Society for Training and Development
Alexandria, Virginia

Edward Schroer
Vice-President, New Business Development
American Society for Training and Development
Alexandria, Virginia

William Shea
Director, Executive Education Relations
Harvard Business School
Harvard University
Boston, Massachusetts

Richard Swanson, *Ph.D.*
Professor, Human Resource Development
Research Center
University of Minnesota
St. Paul, Minnesota
    and
Senior Partner
Swanson & Associates, Inc.
    St. Paul, Minnesota

Mark Van Buren, *Ph.D.*
Senior Research Officer, Research Department
American Society for Training and Development
Alexandria, Virginia

Kevin Wheeler
Director
National Semiconductor University
Santa Clara, California

Additional reviewers:

Claire B. Maurer
Director, Performance Strategies
Bell Atlantic Learning Center
Baltimore, Maryland

Michael F. Cassidy, *Ph.D.*
Associate Professor, Human Resources
Marymount University
Arlington, Virginia

Special thanks to:

Dawn Holley
Research Assistant
Pennsylvania State University

Ning-Li
Research Assistant
Pennsylvania State University

Jean Pritchard
Research Assistant
Pennsylvania State University

◢ SECTION 1   DESCRIPTION OF THE STUDY

This study sought answers to the following questions.

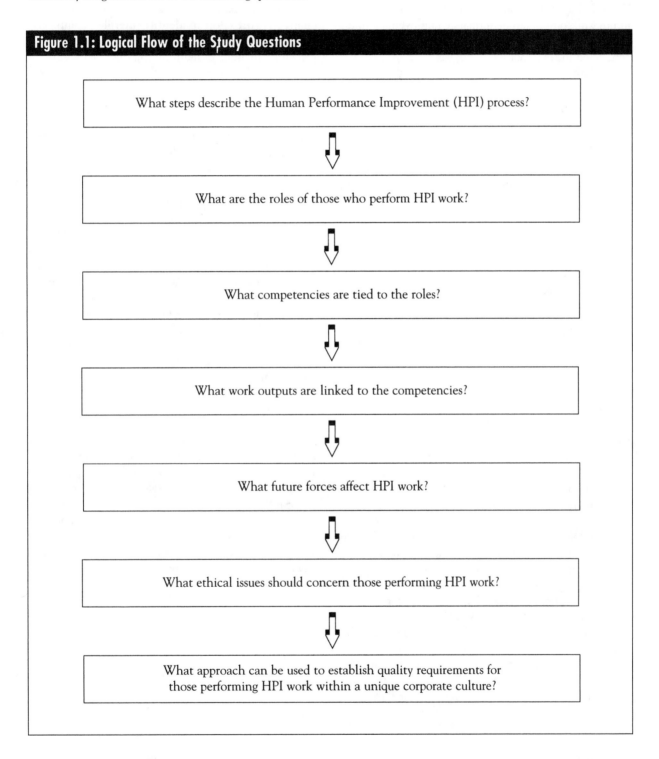

Figure 1.1: Logical Flow of the Study Questions

What steps describe the Human Performance Improvement (HPI) process?

⬇

What are the roles of those who perform HPI work?

⬇

What competencies are tied to the roles?

⬇

What work outputs are linked to the competencies?

⬇

What future forces affect HPI work?

⬇

What ethical issues should concern those performing HPI work?

⬇

What approach can be used to establish quality requirements for those performing HPI work within a unique corporate culture?

Study Methodology

The purpose of this study is to lay the foundation for future work on human performance improvement and is descriptive and exploratory in nature. The study was conducted in three phases.

In Phase I, the study leaders conducted a thorough review of literature on competencies in human resource development, human performance improvement, and related fields. The competencies listed in books, articles, or reports were extracted and compiled into a lengthy list, which was edited to eliminate redundancy.

In Phase II, the list of competencies was circulated to subject matter experts at ASTD headquarters. These subject matter experts then selected the competencies that they believed were most relevant and specific to human performance improvement. The goals of this phase were to

◆ determine the extent of the participants' agreement regarding the competencies

◆ focus the list to include essential competencies needed by those who do human performance improvement work.

When Phase II was completed, the process was repeated in order to verify the list. In this sense, Phase II was a reverse delphi procedure. As Rothwell and Kazanas (1994) explain, "the delphi procedure, named for the ancient Greek oracle of Apollo, was developed by the Rand Corporation and has been widely applied to research problems. Typically, delphi participants are chosen for their special expertise. Participants remain anonymous and never assemble as a group. Instead, information is solicited from them by written survey. The results are compiled by researchers, are fed back to participants with more questions, and this process continues until participants agree on key issues."

Most delphi studies start with a small amount of information that is expanded upon by expert respondents during the delphi process. However, since the experts in Phase II distilled many competencies associated with human performance improvement to those considered most essential, they actually participated in a reverse delphi procedure.

In Phase III, a panel of experts was assembled to review a human performance improvement process model and complete a final round of the reverse delphi process in order to verify the list of competencies associated with human performance improvement work.

Study Limitations

Human performance improvement work is fast-changing. Any effort to identify the roles, competencies, and outputs of this kind of work is fraught with a threefold dilemma of maintaining rigor, achieving results quickly, and requiring frequent—perhaps continuous—updating.

Traditional, empirical research yields valid and reliable results. It maintains rigor. But such research usually takes much time to design and conduct. It also can be expensive. Unfortunately, when traditional and empirically-based approaches are applied to determine the swiftly-changing roles, competencies, and outputs of human performance improvement work, the conclusions when reached are usually too dated to be useful.

On the other hand, nontraditional research yields results that are neither empirically valid nor reliable. While they may strike a responsive chord with users, they lack the defensibility resulting from a rigorous research design. But such studies usually take less time to do and are less expensive than more rigorously conceived and executed research designs.

Since this study design is less complex or methodologically rigorous than empirical research requires, the validity and reliability of the results are simply not as good. Methodological rigor has been sacrificed to a certain extent in order to obtain faster, more current results.

At the heart of this issue is a major challenge facing everyone who does human performance improvement work: How can valid and reliable information be obtained as quickly and as cost-effectively as possible? Rigor may demand elaborate designs and sophisticated analytical approaches; stakeholders and organizational needs may demand prompt, perhaps immediate, results. How can these conflicting issues be resolved satisfactorily to achieve a dynamic balance of rigor and speed?

Units of Analysis

As noted in *Models for HRD Practice* (McLagan, 1989, p. 15), "two key decisions underlie the analysis and description of any work: first, selection of units of analysis; second, determination of the people to whom analysis will apply." The same issues apply to this work as well.

Of course, a unit of analysis refers to the underlying focus of a study. As indicated in *Models for HRD Practice*:

> Job analysis has traditionally focused on behaviors and activities; that is, on what people must do in the course of their work. But there are other options: Job analysis can focus on competencies (the knowledge, skills, values, and attitudes that enable performance), outputs (the products of performance), or results (the consequences of performance).

ASTD Models for Human Performance Improvement is no different. It focuses on roles, competencies, and outputs. But, unlike earlier competency studies, *ASTD Models* derives the roles, competencies, and outputs of HPI work from steps in a human performance improvement process model.

Definition of HPI

Human performance improvement can be synonymous with human performance enhancement, human performance engineering, and human performance consulting. It requires a systematic process of discovering and analyzing important human performance gaps, planning for future improvements in human performance, designing and developing cost-effective and ethically justifiable interventions to close performance gaps, implementing the interventions, and evaluating the financial and nonfinancial results. This definition can be explained as follows:

Systematic means that human performance improvement is approached in an organized, rather than incidental, way. It is based on open systems theory, or the view that any organization is a system that absorbs such environmental *inputs* as people factors, raw materials, capital, and information; uses them in such transformational *processes* as service delivery or manufacturing methods; and expels them as *outputs* such as finished goods or customer services. *Process* is a continuous activity carried out for a purpose.

Discovering and analyzing means identifying and examining present and possible future barriers that prevent an organization, process, or individual from achieving desired results. *Important* implies that priorities are established in the search for improvement opportunities. Importance is influenced by quantity, quality, cost, time, moral or ethical values, or some combination of these elements.

Human performance "denotes a quantified result or a set of obtained results, just as it also refers to the accomplishment, execution, or carrying out of anything ordered or undertaken, to something performed or done, to a deed, achievement, or exploit, and to the execution or accomplishment of the work" (Stolovich & Keeps, 1992, p. 4). Note that the quantifier *human* should be placed in front of *performance* to distinguish it from machine, capital, stock, or other forms of performance. Gaps are the differences between actual and desired results in the past, present, or future.

Planning for future improvements in human performance is meant to emphasize that human performance improvement work is not focused solely on solving past or present problems; rather, it also can be focused on averting future problems or realizing improvement opportunities.

Designing and developing cost-effective and ethically justifiable interventions means finding and formulating optimal or desirable ways of solving past or present human performance problems or planning for future human performance improvement opportunities. The word *intervention* implies a long-term, evolutionary, and progressive change effort. *Cost-effective* implies sensitivity to bottom-line improvements by those who perform human performance improvement work. *Ethically justifiable* implies sensitivity to ethical and moral viewpoints.

Implementing the interventions means finding the optimal—most cost-efficient and cost-effective—way to plan for human performance improvement. Sometimes called *deployment*, it refers to the installation process for a human performance improvement intervention.

Evaluating the results focuses on accountability. Those who do human performance improvement work must always remain keenly aware of the need to gather persuasive evidence of the economic and non-economic value of their efforts.

The Author

William J. Rothwell is professor of human resource development (HRD) in the Department of Adult Education, Instructional Systems, and Workforce Education and Development in the College of Education on the University Park campus of The Pennsylvania State University. In that capacity he directs a graduate program in HRD. He is also director of Penn State's Institute for Research in Training and Development.

Rothwell is author, coauthor, editor, or coeditor of numerous publications, including *ASTD Models for Workplace Learning and Performance* (1999, with Ethan S. Sanders and Jeffrey G. Soper), *The Action Learning Guidebook: A Real-Time Strategy for Problem-Solving, Training Design and Employee Development* (1999, Jossey-Bass/Pfeiffer), *Strategic Human Resource Leader* (1998, with Robert Prescott and Maria Taylor), *Mastering the Instructional Design Process* (2nd ed., 1998, with H.C. Kazanas), and *Beyond Training and Development: State of the Art Strategies for Enhancing Human Performance* (AMACOM, 1996). He holds a Ph.D. from the University of Illinois at Urbana-Champaign and is accredited for life as a senior professional in human resources (SPHR). Rothwell has been a consultant for more than 30 Fortune 500 companies

Human performance technology (HPT) refers to a systematic process that links business strategy and goals—and workers' abilities to achieve them—with a variety of interventions, including education and training. The outcome of this process is improvement in human performance. By requiring close analysis of performance problems or opportunities and their underlying causes, HPT provides effective solutions for any given performance challenge.

Origins of HPT

In September 1988, *Business Week* ran this warning on its cover: "The nation's ability to compete is threatened by inadequate investment in our most important resource: people." That note of urgency around performance and productivity continues to resound within companies both large and small, global and local. Only the ability to recruit, develop, motivate, and retain good performers will sustain the United States' competitive advantage over the long term.

The catch is that building a top-caliber workforce today presents more challenges than it did in the past. Work itself is changing. Jobs aren't as easy to define. Processes and procedures used to be slower and well-documented. People stayed in jobs for a long time and the jobs themselves didn't change much. Not anymore.

Today change is happening faster than ever before. Work environments, operations, job functions, and processes are much more interdependent. Job, customer, and technological requirements seem to change almost daily as organizations scurry to deliver goods and services at a faster rate, with quality improvements, and at a lower cost.

For many organizations, these key challenges prompted training solutions that spanned the gamut of possibilities, from on-line learning to union-guaranteed professional development programs.

By some estimates, U.S. businesses are spending upwards of $50 billion annually on formal training. However, it's clear that training alone isn't always the best means to achieving performance goals. The challenge is to blend learning with other effective interventions in a more comprehensive manner.

In 1988, Rummler and Brache referred to training as a "piecemeal" approach, adding that "Whether the concern is quality, customer focus, productivity, cycle time or cost, the underlying issue is performance." HPT is the tool businesses can use to enhance productivity and organizational capability in a sustained and meaningful way. Combined with learning and instructional technology, HPT provides a strategy for focusing directly on performance improvement.

In 1992, work by Rosenberg, Coscarelli, and Hutchison noted that HPT evolved from these areas:

Systems. In 1988, Robert Mager discussed the use of systems as a framework for implementing HPT. He said that instructional technology may serve as a sub-system of HPT and HPT as a subsystem of a company's management structure. Two years later Peter Senge described systems thinking as essential to building a learning organization, adding that improving individual performance requires a framework to view "patterns of change rather than static 'snapshots.'"

Behavioral and cognitive psychology and instructional systems design. The roots of HPT stem from behavioral and cognitive psychology, which provide a theoretical basis for how people learn. In fact, behavioral and cognitive psychologists such as Skinner, Crowder, Gilbert, Bloom, Glasser, Bruner, and Gagné established the fundamentals for programmed instruction and instructional technology.

Analytical systems. These systems provide a structure for diagnosing performance problems. As early as 1960, pioneers such as Mager, Gilbert, Rummler, and Harless used newly developed analysis techniques to show that training and instruction may not always improve performance. Their work became a catalyst in the search for effective performance improvement measures, which, in turn, led to the development of the performance technology movement.

Ways to Improve Performance

Practitioners in the developing field of HPT soon began to investigate the many options—including training—for improving performance. They found that the best way to understand these options is to examine the three aspects of performance that can be changed.

First, we're able to change the actual work an employee performs—his or her job, the things they do. Making changes in this area could involve restructuring organizations, changing manufacturing processes, dividing up or combining jobs, or using quality management approaches.

The workplace itself also is an aspect that we can change. For example, it's possible to create better work environments; provide better resources, tools, and information; and offer enhancements such as telecommuting. And finally, we can change the makeup of the workforce by hiring, replacing, transferring, or training people.

A slightly modified version of Gilbert's Behavior Engineering Model (1978) provides six performance improvement factors for enhancing individual, group, and organizational performance in these three areas. The six factors are

◆ consequences, incentives, and rewards
◆ data and information
◆ resources, tools, and environmental support
◆ individual capacity
◆ motives and expectations
◆ skills and knowledge.

Consequences, incentives, and rewards are all forms of motivation that can have a positive and negative effect on performance. Well-trained employees may not perform if they believe they're not receiving adequate compensation. In some cases, poor performance reaps rewards. For example, though a company may want its salespeople to move into territory already served by the competition, training may not change their behavior if they continue to receive higher compensation for selling in established areas.

Sometimes all that a performer may need in order to improve is data and information. The company simply specifies the level of performance it expects and explains what isn't acceptable. This low-cost intervention may involve job or performance standards to indicate the level of proficiency expected; feedback from supervisors, peers, or customers; and performance or job documentation and job aids, in print or on-line.

Resources, tools, and environmental support can have an enormous impact on performance, and it's management's job to provide these things. Even well-trained, motivated employees will deliver substandard performances if they don't have the staff, money, time, or materials they need. For example, why train employees on new software if their department can't afford that software? This may actually cause morale and demotivation problems. Providing an environment where high performance can flourish and be a rewarding, enjoyable experience requires commitment, support, and leadership from all levels of management.

Another critical area is the overall design of the job and the organization. Sometimes the inefficiencies of a job or the bureaucracy of an organization can inhibit high-quality performance.

In some cases, tools, incentives, and support may be there, but the individual performer's capabilities may be lacking. Matching people to jobs is a complicated process that takes into account a great deal of personal information such as educational history, interests and traits, career plans, and academic and physical capabilities. Despite careful analysis, mismatches can happen, and, sometimes, no performance improvement intervention can make a difference in how the person performs. The problem may call for redesigning the job,

splitting it, or adding more staff to do it. It also is wise to tighten procedures for assessing applicants' qualifications instead of trying to train poorly qualified candidates. Job reassignment or termination, when warranted, are other options.

Employees' motives and expectations—how they view themselves and their jobs—also are critical to performing well. An employee with high self-esteem, sound ethics, and socially accepted values is more likely to perform to standard, while an individual's fear of failure, punishment, and risk taking can create obstacles. For example, the best resources and compensation package probably won't inspire a salesperson who is afraid of rejection.

Lack of skills and knowledge contributes to substandard performance. Education and training play as important a role in improving performance as effective motivation, clear performance standards, resources, tools, support, ability, and motives. As the information needs of businesses expand, fast, effective learning is now more important than ever before.

An HPT Model

Although there are many sound approaches to HPT, each involves the steps and activities of a performance improvement process or system that includes performance analysis, cause analysis, and intervention selection as shown in the generic model in Figure 2.1.

Performance Analysis

Performance analysis is the process of identifying the organization's performance requirements and comparing them to its objectives and capabilities. In 1986, Harless described this as "front-end analysis."

This kind of analysis is essential because it attempts to identify what must be done to correct a specific performance problem (e.g., diminishing productivity, growing number of errors, falling sales). Or it may identify an opportunity for improving such performance as applying a new technology.

According to Rossett (1988), the goal of performance analysis is to measure the gap between the desired and actual performance. An organization uses a careful assessment of customer needs to develop such workforce requirements as competencies and abilities for achieving organizational goals. These requirements determine the desired performance. To measure the actual performance, the organization then conducts a comprehensive assessment of its employees' current capabilities, the efficiency of its organizational structure, and its competitive position. The result of the analysis is

Figure 2.1: A Performance Technology Model

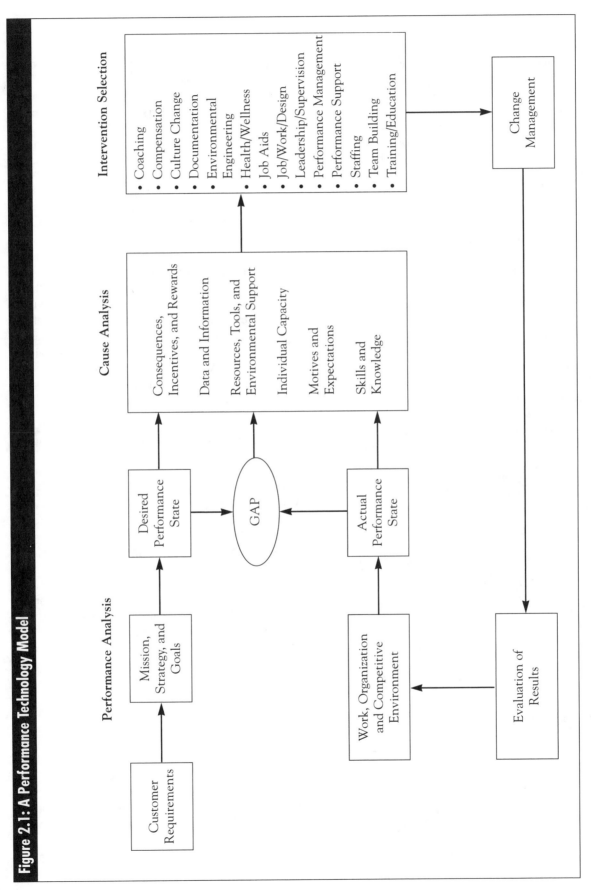

Performance Analysis

Customer Requirements → Mission, Strategy, and Goals → Desired Performance State

Work, Organization and Competitive Environment → Actual Performance State

Desired Performance State → GAP ← Actual Performance State

Cause Analysis

- Consequences, Incentives, and Rewards
- Data and Information
- Resources, Tools, and Environmental Support
- Individual Capacity
- Motives and Expectations
- Skills and Knowledge

Intervention Selection

- Coaching
- Compensation
- Culture Change
- Documentation
- Environmental Engineering
- Health/Wellness
- Job Aids
- Job/Work/Design
- Leadership/Supervision
- Performance Management
- Performance Support
- Staffing
- Team Building
- Training/Education

Change Management

Evaluation of Results

Deterline, W.A. and Rosenberg, M.J. (1992). *Workplace Productivity: Performance Technology Success Stories*. Washington, DC: International Society for Performance Improvement.

to identify the gap between the desired and actual performance levels. The HPT practitioner's job is to determine what interventions or combination of interventions will close that gap, bringing the actual in line with the desired performance level.

For example, a company planning to develop a new product may have completed customer requirement surveys and used the data to form its business strategy and to pin down tasks, competencies, and productivity levels for specific jobs in product design, manufacturing, marketing, sales, and service. But close examination may reveal a gap between employees' actual capabilities and the company's workforce needs for creating and delivering the product.

What's more, different sections of the workforce may be stronger in some skills than others. The salesforce may have experience selling a similar product, but the product design team may not have the necessary background to do its part. In this instance, the performance analysis can pinpoint the more serious gaps in performance, so the company can concentrate its investments in the areas that require the most improvement.

In 1987, Rossett noted the variety of tools and techniques that can be used to conduct a performance analysis—reviews of organizational information, interviews, focus groups, and observations from subject matter experts, customers, suppliers, and performers. She also advised gauging the feelings of such key stakeholders as senior management and supervisors in regard to performance problems and related solutions. Peoples' attitudes can influence their perception of how important a problem is, the value of solving it, and the likelihood of succeeding with the particular solution.

Cause Analysis

Moving hastily to adopt a solution or intervention—such as training—is a common mistake made during the performance improvement process. The fact is, even when the performance analysis is complete, it still may be too soon to plan a solution because the analysis may have only identified symptoms of the problem. Poor sales, for example, may only be a symptom. The underlying cause may have more to do with the competitors' underpricing strategy than with a need to train salespeople.

To find out what's behind a problem requires cause analysis, the second phase of HPT. It bridges performance analysis, which measures the performance gap, with selection of the best interventions to boost performance and to reduce or eliminate the performance gap.

A cause analysis may show that the salesforce is well trained to sell a new product and that the product has received high marks from industry experts. The price may be competitive as well. But further investigation may show that the salespeople are better compensated for selling an older, more established product than the new one—and that alone is the underlying cause for poor sales. Here any training intervention would be inappropriate and a waste of resources and staff.

Intervention Selection

Most times improvement calls for a combination of interventions, because as Rummler notes (in Dixon, 1988), performance problems are often "multi-causal." Training—combined with on-the-job support in the form of effective tools, documentation, and other related resources—is more likely to be successful and effective. The rate of success and effectiveness increases further if management is willing to engage in the training and provide the workforce with post-training support.

In 1992, Spitzer suggested 11 intervention design principles for promoting successful interventions. They are summarized as follows:

◆ Base designs on a comprehensive understanding of the entire issue. This is why performance and cause analysis phases are critical to designing an appropriate intervention.
◆ Carefully target interventions. While it is important to select the right people for an intervention, it's just as important to be sure that the intervention will yield results worth the investment in time, people, and resources.
◆ Find a sponsor for the intervention. Unlike a client or customer, the sponsor makes the largest financial and organizational commitment to the project. According to Zemke (in Dixon, 1988), "The farther up the organization you have to go to find out why the problem is worth fixing, the more likely it will get fixed; or at least someone will be willing to spend some money trying to fix it."
◆ Use teams to design interventions. As an interdisciplinary approach, HPT requires expertise in many areas covering the various types of performance problems of organizations and individuals. It's difficult to find one person who alone possesses all the needed skills and knowledge.
◆ Design cost-effective interventions. The lowest-cost solution that effectively corrects the performance problem is the best choice.
◆ Design interventions based on what's most important, most possible, and most needed.

◆ Consider using existing programs or off-the-shelf products that fit your needs before incurring the cost of designing an intervention.

◆ Try to make the intervention as comprehensive as possible with the resources you have. Short-term, simplistic solutions may only bring customer dissatisfaction later.

◆ Ensure that interventions are sustainable over a long period of time. The best way to do this is to integrate them fully into the organization's culture and operations.

◆ Focus on development and implementation when designing an intervention. The only interventions worth recommending are those you can actually create and apply.

◆ Use an interactive approach when designing interventions. Trials and constant revision are your keys to getting it right.

Types of Interventions

There are dozens of interventions, and because many of them have similar qualities, it can be confusing to sort them out. One of the best ways to think about interventions and to work with them is to organize them by category. Rosenberg (1990) suggested four major categories of interventions:

Human resources development. Here the focus is on improving individual employee performance using training, career development, individual feedback, incentives, and rewards.

Organizational development. This category centers on improving the performance of groups or teams. It involves organizational design, team building, culture change, group feedback, incentives, and rewards.

Human resource management. Here the concern is with coaching and managing individual and group performance, as well as recruiting and staffing. Intervention topics include supervision, leadership, succession planning, and personnel selection.

Environmental engineering. Here the focus is on providing tools and facilities for improving performance. Examples include ergonomics, job aids, electronic resources, systems design, job and organizational design, and facilities design.

Implementation

Implementation of the solution is as important a stage as the analysis and deserves as much time and careful planning. A good solution that's poorly implemented becomes a poor solution.

Change management is a critical aspect for successful implementation. This is because HPT interventions often cause some kind of change affecting the organization or the individual. If organizational change isn't addressed adequately, implementation may fail.

Resistance to change—particularly changes that affect performance—can be a powerful obstacle. People who do human performance improvement work, senior management, and employees themselves should help everyone involved to move from avoiding change to accepting it.

Evaluation

After applying or implementing the HPT solution, it's important to monitor it to determine its effect on performance improvement and on the organization. Kirkpatrick's four levels of evaluation (1975) provide guidelines for developing a comprehensive strategy for assessing the intervention's effectiveness.

First, note reactions from employees, managers, customers, and suppliers. What are their impressions of how the intervention has affected them? Next, look at learning and capability. Find out if people are able to do more after the intervention than before it, if they have more skill or knowledge than they did before.

Then determine whether employees are exhibiting a higher level of performance in their jobs. Look to see if the intervention(s) has affected the way employees are doing their jobs, and what they are accomplishing. Are they using the new skills, tools, processes, and other resources in their work?

Finally, concentrate on results. Determine the impact of the intervention on the performance gap. It should change for the better in ways that have a positive correlation to business performance and bottom-line concerns.

Evaluative data help to identify changes in the actual performance of the workforce, determine if the gap between actual and desired performance has closed, and verify the "value" of the intervention in the form of worthwhile accomplishments. This valuable information is key to measuring the effectiveness of HPT solutions.

Adapted from Rosenberg, M. J. "From training to performance: Human performance technology." In R. L. Craig (ed.), Training and Development Handbook, 4th edition. New York: McGraw-Hill, 1996.

The Author

Marc J. Rosenberg is a senior consultant with OmniTech Consulting Group, Inc., in New Jersey. His career includes 18 years in management positions with AT&T where he developed the company's education and training strategy and directed major corporate initiatives in learning technology, performance management, and education and training reengineering. He holds a doctorate in instructional design, and has degrees in communications and marketing.

Rosenberg is a past president of the International Society for Performance Improvement; a founding editorial board member of *Performance Improvement Quarterly*; co-editor of ISPI's *Performance Technology: Success Stories* (1992); and a contributing author to the *Handbook of Human Performance Technology* (1992 and 1999), as well as the American Society for Training and Development's (ASTD) *Training and Development Handbook* (4th edition).

He is the recipient of numerous awards for his professional service and contributions in the areas of training, performance management, and electronic performance support. His expertise extends across all of the emerging fields of knowledge management, multimedia, inter-intranet, and performance support technologies.

◢ SECTION 3   FUTURE FORCES

The following trends in performance, business, learning, organizational structure, and technology are the future forces that are expected to influence and change the way we work.

Performance

- A paradigm shift is underway in the training field that requires training professionals to shift their focus from such traditional development inputs as classes and hours to such outputs as performance at the individual, team, and organizational levels.
- Corporate training functions are under growing pressure to demonstrate their organizational value in these terms.
- The shift from training to performance is beginning to manifest itself in changing titles, changing perceptions, and changing skill requirements for trainers.
- Trainers are taking an active role in helping employees make the transition to new team-based, high-involvement structures and practices. Employees need training in group dynamics and interpersonal relations, in understanding information about their performance and the financial performance of the business, and in systems thinking in order to better understand how all the parts of their organization fit together and affect one another.
- There is a focus on skill standards, measurement and evaluation, and testing in the workplace.
- Currently, most training organizations evaluate only a few of their courses for performance improvement at the individual or organizational level.
- The shift to human performance improvement holds great potential for transforming training in companies and increasing its value to the organization.

Business Trends

- As a whole, America's workforce is becoming (1) more diverse, with growing shares of both Hispanic and Asian workers, (2) older, as the Baby-Boom generation nears retirement, and (3) less prepared for the jobs that are being created in this new economy.
- Workers with the lowest levels of education are experiencing dramatic declines in their inflation-adjusted earnings, while workers with high levels of education are enjoying modest increases in their wages.
- Growth in the number of workers who are employed on a temporary or contingent basis is expected to continue into the early part of the next century.
- Job tenure actually has declined for one influential group of workers—males over the age of 40.
- Average hourly wages continue to fall for the majority of workers.

- It is in the interest of both workers and employers for there to be an increase in the level of training.

Learning

- Building a learning organization is still considered important within the business community.
- The challenge for training professionals in corporations is to operationalize the concepts of a learning organization.

Technology

- Traditional classroom delivery is still predominant in corporate training.
- The use of technology-based training delivery is increasing immensely.
- Reductions in cost and improvements in reliability of these technologies have spurred entire industries in multimedia and communications technology to take off in recent years.
- Increased use of technology is being driven by many forces within companies. Among these forces are (1) the decline in the size of training departments, (2) reductions in product manufacturing cycle time, (3) cutbacks in employee travel, (4) less tolerance for time away from the job for training, and (5) the need to keep employees updated with ever-increasing skill requirements.
- Trainers must learn the appropriate situations and content suitable for each learning platform.
- One major implication of this shift toward technology-based learning is the need for training professionals to work in tandem with technical experts to develop such systems. Evidence from companies indicates the growing need for training organizations to partner with their Information Technology and Information Systems departments. In many cases these departments are leading the way in developing expert systems and electronic performance support systems (EPSS), as well as delivering training via computer networks.
- Two barriers to the widespread implementation of technology-based training are the inability to demonstrate the value of the technology to line managers and the lack of expertise to develop such systems.

Structure of Training Organizations

◆ Training and human resource departments are being downsized, restructured, outsourced, and generally asked to do more with less.

◆ Instruction is located closer to the work site in order to reduce costs and deliver training in a more flexible environment.

◆ Corporate training organizations frequently are being realigned along with strategic business units.

◆ Training suppliers—from sole proprietors to community colleges and universities—are emerging, in many cases, as the training supplier of choice.

◆ A new set of challenges exists for corporate trainers, who increasingly find themselves responsible for (1) purchasing training from outside, (2) creating structures to support networks of both internal and external training providers, (3) acting as brokers of learning services, (4) negotiating contracts and "make-or-buy" analyses, and (5) developing "train-the-trainer" courses.

Adapted from Trends That Affect Corporate Learning & Performance, *2d edition, American Society for Training and Development, April 1996.*

The Author

Michele Brock is currently a consultant in the Center for Performance Improvement, Pricewaterhouse-Coopers, LLP. Formerly she was a project manager with the American Society for Training & Development. Brock has master's degrees in Industrial Organizational Psychology from the University of Baltimore and in Human Performance Systems from Marymount University.

This section introduces a model of the human performance improvement process. The model was adapted from a variety of sources, including Warner Burke, Geary Rummler, the ASTD Expert Advisory Panel, the ASTD Board of Directors, the ASTD Council of Governors, the International Society for Performance Improvement model, William Bramer, Joe Harless, Jim Robinson, Dana Gaines Robinson, Richard Swanson, Robert Mager, Marc Rosenberg, and Paul Elliott.

Steps in a Human Performance Improvement Process

There are six core steps in the human performance improvement process. They are depicted in Figure 4.1 and are described as follows:

Step 1: Performance analysis. At this point, people who do human performance improvement work identify and describe past, present, and future human performance gaps. Performance analysis is carried out by collecting information to answer such questions as:

◆ What is the desired performance situation versus the actual situation?

◆ What is the performance gap or difference?

◆ Who is affected by the performance gap? Is it one person, a group, an organization, or a work process?

◆ When and where did the performance gap first occur—or when and where is it expected to begin?

◆ When and where were its effects, side effects (symptoms), and after effects (consequences) first noticed? Have they been noticed consistently or inconsistently?

◆ How has the gap been affecting the organization? Have the effects been widespread or limited? Is the performance gap traceable to individuals, work groups, locations, departments, divisions, suppliers, distributors, customers, or others? What are the immediate and direct results of the gap?

◆ How much has the gap cost the organization? How can the tangible economic impact of the gap best be calculated? How can the intangible impact of the gap be calculated in lost customer goodwill or worker morale?

The outcome of performance analysis should be a clear description of the existing and desired conditions surrounding performance. As such, the analysis can answer four key questions:

◆ What results (performance outcomes) are being achieved?

◆ What results are desired?

◆ How large is the performance gap?

◆ What is the impact of the performance gap?

Step 2: Cause analysis. At this point the root causes of a past, present, or future performance gap are identified. In other words, the question, "Why does the performance gap exist?" is answered. To determine the causes of performance gaps, those who do human performance improvement work should consider the following issues (Gilbert, 1978; Gilbert, 1982a & 1982b):

◆ How well do performers see the results or consequences of what they do? Performance gaps can, of course, result when performers do not see how their work helps to meet organizational, work process, team, or other performers' needs.

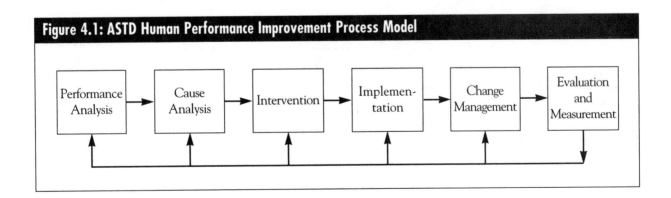

Figure 4.1: ASTD Human Performance Improvement Process Model

Performance Analysis → Cause Analysis → Intervention → Implementation → Change Management → Evaluation and Measurement

- How well are performers rewarded or provided with incentives for performing as desired? How well do incentives (offered before performance) or rewards (offered after performance) serve to induce performers to achieve desired work results? Are performers penalized or otherwise given disincentives for achieving desired work results?
- How well are people given the data, information, or feedback they need to perform at the time they need it? Are performers given important information they need to perform on a timely basis?
- How well are performers supported in what they do by appropriate environmental support, resources, equipment, or tools? Do performers have the necessary job aids and working conditions to perform?
- How well are individuals or groups able to perform? Do employees have the ability, time, and other resources necessary to perform?
- How well are performers motivated to perform, and how realistic are their expectations? Do performers want to achieve desired results? What payoffs do they expect? How realistic are their expectations?

- How well do performers' knowledge and skills match up to performance demands? Could performers achieve desired results if their lives depended on it, or do they lack the necessary know-how?

Cause analysis can be carried out using many tools and techniques. One approach is to ask performers to trace the causes of a performance gap using a fishbone diagram similar to the one shown in Figure 4.2. Whatever methods are used, the outcome of cause analysis should be a clear description of the cause(s) of the performance gaps.

Cause Analysis Fishbone Diagram

Directions: Ask performers, process owners, performers' managers, and other stakeholders to analyze the root causes of a performance gap using the following diagram. In a meeting or team setting, ask them to describe the performance gap in the box shown on the far right in Figure 4.2. They should clarify as much as possible what is actually happening and what results are desired. Then, ask them to examine the cause of this gap by considering each issue described in the boxes to the left of the performance gap box. There are no "right" or "wrong" answers in any absolute sense, of course.

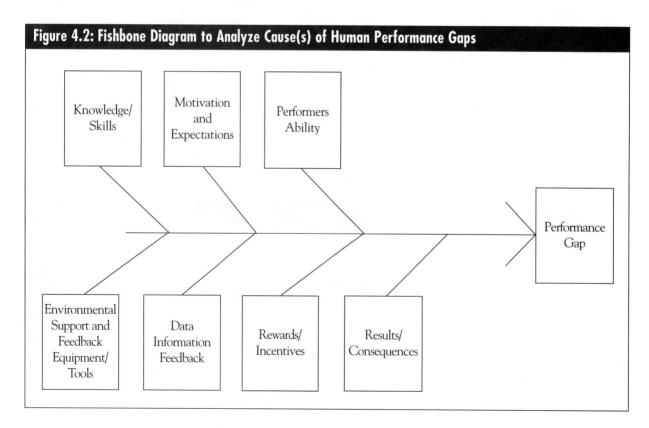

Figure 4.2: Fishbone Diagram to Analyze Cause(s) of Human Performance Gaps

This model is adapted from Thomas Gilbert's Behavioral Engineering Model.

Step 3: Selection of appropriate interventions. Here people who do human performance work consider possible ways to close past, present, or possible future performance gaps by addressing their root cause(s). Interventions may be used individually or in combination, depending on the cause(s) of the gap(s).

Step 4: Implementation. At this point, people who do human performance improvement work help the organization prepare to install an intervention. Among other issues, they may help performers, performers' managers, process owners, and other stakeholders to:

- examine what the organization currently is doing to address the cause(s) of the human performance gap
- determine what the organization should do in the future to address the cause(s) of the human performance gap
- assess changes inside or outside the organization that may affect the intervention as it is implemented
- clarify and emphasize how the intervention will help the organization meet its needs, achieve its mission, and realize its strategic planning goals and objectives
- identify the best sources of talent and resources to implement the intervention.

The results of this step usually are a clear sense of the desired outcomes to be achieved from the intervention, an action plan that enjoys the ownership of key stakeholders, and the assembly of talent necessary to implement the intervention. To be effective, any intervention requires a long-term commitment and constant oversight by those who do human performance improvement work as well as by stakeholders and decision makers.

Step 5: Change management. During this step, people who do human performance improvement work should monitor the intervention as it is being implemented. They consider such questions as:

- How well is the intervention addressing the root cause(s) of human performance gaps?
- What measurable improvements can be shown?
- How much ownership have stakeholders vested in the intervention, and what steps can be taken to improve that ownership?
- How are changing conditions inside and outside the organization affecting the intervention?

The outcome of this step is usually an intervention that is managed on a regular basis in a way consistent with desired results.

Step 6: Evaluation and measurement. At this point, those conducting human performance improvement work take stock of the results achieved by the intervention. They consider such questions as:

- How well did the intervention achieve desired and measurable results?
- How well realized were the forecasted and measurable improvements targeted for the intervention?
- What were the positive and negative side effects? What side effects of the intervention were noticeable?
- What lessons were learned from the intervention that could be applied in the future?
- How well has the intervention been adopted in the corporate culture?
- What best practices or lessons learned resulted from the intervention?

Evaluation is properly targeted at the subject for change (such as employee performance) and at the intervention (the means to an end.) As such, it answers these key questions:

- Did results match intentions?
- Was a human performance gap solved or a human performance improvement opportunity realized?
- Were organizational needs met?

Measurement determines how much change and how much improvement occurred. It answers the following questions:

- What were the impacts of the intervention strategy?
- What value was added in economic and noneconomic terms?

The Author

William J. Rothwell is professor of human resource development in the Department of Adult Education, Instructional Systems, and Workforce Education and Development at the University Park campus of Pennsylvania State University. Rothwell is also director of the Institute for Research in Training and Development at Penn State.

What roles, competencies, and outputs are associated with the human performance improvement process model? How can measurable quality requirements be established for people who do human performance improvement work? This section answers these important questions, and, therefore, is the heart of this study.

Roles Tied to the HPI Process Model

As work is reengineered, organizations require individuals to take on a broader array of duties and responsibilities than might be implied by traditional job descriptions. That trend can be seen in the emergence of self-directed work teams, in which all members are expected to meet all team responsibilities. Instead of jobs or positions, then, a proper emphasis should be placed on *roles*, understood to mean the parts played by people as they do their work. Just as actors and actresses assume roles in theatrical productions, so too are roles assumed by people who do human performance improvement work.

Four roles may be inferred in part from the steps in the human performance improvement process model:

◆ **Analyst**—conducts troubleshooting to isolate the cause(s) of human performance gaps or identifies areas in which human performance can be improved

◆ **Intervention specialist**—selects appropriate interventions to address the root cause(s) of performance gaps

◆ **Change manager**—ensures that interventions are implemented in ways consistent with desired results and that they help individuals and groups achieve results

◆ **Evaluator**—assesses the impact of interventions and follows up on changes made, actions taken, and results achieved in order to provide participants and stakeholders with information about how well interventions are being implemented.

Figure 5.1: Relationship Between the Human Performance Improvement Process and Roles

Human Performance Improvement Process Model	Human Performance Improvement Roles
Performance Analysis	
Cause Analysis	Analyst
Interventions	Intervention Specialist
Implementation	
Change Management	Change Manager
Evaluation and Measurement	Evaluator

There is a relationship between the steps in the human performance improvement process model and the roles of people who do human performance improvement work. While expert mastery of all roles is not expected of those doing human performance improvement work, the general relationship between the human performance improvement process and the four roles is depicted in Figure 5.1 on page 17.

Competencies Associated with HPI Work

Competencies are "internal capabilities that people bring to their jobs. They may be expressed in a broad, even infinite, array of on-the-job behaviors" (McLagan, 1989, p. 77). They are identified by examining exemplary performers, not by studying work duties or responsibilities. Following is a list of competencies needed by those who perform human performance improvement work.

Core competencies. There are 15 competencies essential to all roles and across all steps in the human performance improvement process.

1. **Industry awareness:** understanding the vision, strategy, goals, and culture of an industry; linking human performance improvement interventions to organizational goals.
2. **Leadership skills:** knowing how to lead or influence others positively to achieve desired work results.
3. **Interpersonal relationship skills:** working effectively with others to achieve common goals and exercising effective interpersonal influence.
4. **Technological awareness and understanding:** using existing or new technology and different types of software and hardware; understanding performance support systems and applying them as appropriate.
5. **Problem-solving skills:** detecting performance gaps and helping other people discover ways to close the performance gaps in the present and future; closing performance gaps between actual and ideal performance.
6. **Systems thinking and understanding:** identifying inputs, throughputs, and outputs of a subsystem, system, or suprasystem and applying that information to improve human performance; realizing the implications of interventions on many parts of an organization, process, or individual; taking steps to address any side effects of human performance improvement interventions.
7. **Performance understanding:** distinguishing between activities and results; recognizing implications, outcomes, and consequences.

8. **Knowledge of interventions:** demonstrating an understanding of the many ways that human performance can be improved in organizational settings; showing how to apply specific human performance improvement interventions to close existing or anticipated performance gaps.
9. **Business understanding:** demonstrating awareness of the inner workings of business functions and how business decisions affect financial or nonfinancial work results (McLagan, 1989).
10. **Organization understanding:** seeing organizations as dynamic, political, economic, and social systems that have multiple goals; using this larger perspective as a framework for understanding and influencing events and change (McLagan, 1989).
11. **Negotiating/contracting skills:** organizing, preparing, overseeing, and evaluating work performed by vendors, contingent workers, or outsourcing agents.
12. **Buy-in/advocacy skills:** building ownership or support for change among affected individuals, groups, and other stakeholders.
13. **Coping skills:** knowing how to deal with ambiguity and how to handle the stress resulting from change and from multiple meanings or possibilities.
14. **Ability to see "big picture":** looking beyond details to see overarching goals and results.
15. **Consulting skills:** understanding the results that stakeholders desire from a process and providing insight into how efficiently and effectively those results can be achieved.

Competencies Associated with HPI Roles

There are also specific competencies associated with each role played by those involved in HPI work. They are listed as follows:

Role 1: Analyst

16. **Performance analysis skills (front-end analysis):** the process of comparing actual and ideal performance in order to identify performance gaps or opportunities.
17. **Needs analysis survey design and development skills (open-ended and structured):** preparing written (mail), oral (phone), or electronic (e-mail) surveys using open-ended (essay) and closed (scaled) questions in order to identify human performance improvement needs.
18. **Competency identification skills:** identifying the knowledge and skill requirements of teams, jobs, tasks, roles, and work (McLagan, 1989).
19. **Questioning skills:** gathering pertinent information to stimulate insight in individuals and groups through use of interviews and other probing methods (McLagan, 1989).

20. **Analytical skills (synthesis):** breaking down the components of a larger whole and reassembling them to achieve improved human performance.

21. **Work environment analytical skills:** examining work environments for issues or characteristics affecting human performance.

Role 2: Intervention Specialist

22. **Performance information interpretation skills:** finding useful meaning from the results of performance analysis and helping performers, performers' managers, process owners, and other stakeholders to do so.

23. **Intervention selection skills:** selecting human performance improvement interventions that address the root cause(s) of performance gaps rather than symptoms or side effects.

24. **Performance change interpretation skills:** forecasting and analyzing the effects of interventions and their consequences.

25. **Ability to assess relationships among interventions:** examining the effects of multiple human performance improvement interventions on parts of an organization, as well as the effects on the organization's interactions with customers, suppliers, distributors, and workers.

26. **Ability to identify critical business issues and changes:** determining key business issues and applying that information during the implementation of a human performance improvement intervention.

27. **Goal implementation skills:** ensuring that goals are converted effectively into actions to close existing or pending performance gaps; getting results despite conflicting priorities, lack of resources, or ambiguity.

Role 3: Change Manager

28. **Change impetus skills:** determining what the organization should do to address the cause(s) of a human performance gap at present and in the future.

29. **Communication channel, informal network, and alliance understanding:** knowing how communication moves through an organization by various channels, networks, and alliances; building such channels, networks, and alliances to achieve improvements in productivity and performance.

30. **Group dynamics process understanding:** understanding how groups function; influencing people so that group, work, and individual needs are addressed (McLagan, 1989).

31. **Process consultation skills:** observing individuals and groups for their interactions and the effects of their interactions with others.

32. **Facilitation skills:** helping performers, performers' managers, process owners, and stakeholders to discover new insights.

Role 4: Evaluator

33. **Performance gap evaluation skills:** measuring or helping others to measure the difference between actual and ideal performance.

34. **Ability to evaluate results against organizational goals:** assessing how well the results of a human performance improvement intervention match intentions.

35. **Standard setting skills:** measuring desired results of organizations, processes, or individuals; helping others to establish and measure work expectations.

36. **Ability to assess impact on culture:** examining the effects of human performance gaps and human performance improvement interventions on shared beliefs and assumptions about "right" and "wrong" ways of behaving and acting in one organizational setting.

37. **Human performance improvement intervention reviewing skills:** finding ways to evaluate and continuously improve human performance improvement interventions before and during implementation.

38. **Feedback skills:** collecting information about performance and feeding it back clearly, specifically, and on a timely basis to affected individuals or groups (McLagan, 1989).

Outputs Associated with Each HPI Competency/Role

An *output* is "a product or service that an individual or group delivers to others, especially to colleagues, customers, or clients" (McLagan, 1989, p. 77). The human performance improvement process model and the roles related to it logically imply outputs. As in McLagan's 1989 work, "a particular job may involve responsibility for many of these work outputs or only a few" (p. 18).

In *ASTD Models for Human Performance Improvement*, there are two kinds of outputs: enabling and terminal. An *enabling output* is linked directly to a competency. It is an output associated with the demonstration of that competency. A *terminal output*, on the other hand, is linked directly to a role. It is the final outcome associated with that role.

Lists of outputs associated with the core competencies and the roles of people who do human performance improvement work are provided in Tables 5.1 and 5.2. Of course, the lists represent menus of choices. Not every output must be demonstrated for each competency or role or by any one person who does human performance improvement work.

Table 5.1: Enabling Outputs Associated with HPI Core Competencies

Core Competencies	Enabling Outputs
Industry Awareness: understanding the vision, strategy, goals, and culture of an industry; linking human performance improvement interventions to organizational goals	• Descriptions of industry/organizational status
Leadership Skills: knowing how to lead or influence others positively to achieve desired work results	• Positive influence on others exhibited
Interpersonal Relationship Skills: working effectively with others to achieve common goals and exercising effective interpersonal influence	• Positive relationships established and maintained with clients, stakeholders, and decision makers
Technological Awareness and Understanding: using existing or new technology and different types of software and hardware; understanding performance support systems and applying them as appropriate	• Facility in using technology • Criteria for choosing optimal or cost-effective technology • Selection of appropriate technology • Designs for establishing, implementing, or evaluating performance support systems • Designs for integrating the work people do and the technology used to achieve desired results • Environmental scans for appropriate technology
Problem-Solving Skills: detecting performance gaps and helping other people discover ways to close the performance gaps in the present and future; closing performance gaps between actual and ideal performance	• Strategies for groups, teams, or individuals to discover, present, or anticipate performance gaps • Application of quality tools to identify special and general causes of problems (histograms, trend charts, etc.) • Written and oral briefings to performers, performers' managers, process owners, and other stakeholders about performance gaps • Problem-solving activities to lead performers, performers' managers, process owners, and other stakeholders to discover/forecast the likely impact of multiple interventions on processes, individuals, or the organization
Systems Thinking and Understanding: identifying inputs, throughputs, and outputs of a subsystem, system, or suprasystem and applying that information to improve human performance; realizing the implications of interventions on many parts of an organization, process, or individual; taking steps to address any side effects of human performance improvement interventions	• Systems flow charts showing the impact of interventions on processes, individuals, or the organization
Performance Understanding: distinguishing between activities and results; recognizing implications, outcomes, and consequences	• Written and oral descriptions of performance • Visual charts, process descriptions, or other aids to show performance

Core Competencies	Enabling Outputs
Knowledge of Interventions: demonstrating an understanding of the many ways that human performance can be improved in organizational settings; showing how to apply specific human performance improvement interventions to close existing or anticipated performance gaps	**Plans for:** • Employee recruitment or selection programs • Employee orientation programs • Employee training programs using systematic approaches • Establishing learning organizations • Employee performance appraisal practices and programs • Career development programs • Organization development interventions • Compensation, reward, and incentive programs • Employee feedback programs • Employee discipline programs • Employee counseling and wellness programs • Safety programs • Improved tools and equipment • Improved on-the-job training • Improved on-the-job learning • Job aids • Organizational design • Job design • Task design • Ergonomic improvements • Improved employee staff planning and forecasting programs • Other human performance improvement strategies/interventions
Business Understanding: demonstrating awareness of the inner workings of business functions and how business decisions affect financial or nonfinancial work results (McLagan, 1989)	• Flow charts of work processes • Flow charts of organizational operations/networks • Flow charts of interactions with customers and other stakeholders • Cash flow statements • Budget documents • Income sheets and balance statements
Organization Understanding: seeing organizations as dynamic, political, economic, and social systems that have multiple goals; using this larger perspective as a framework for understanding and influencing events and change (McLagan, 1989)	• Stories about organizational culture/history and experiences • Descriptions of the likely impact of changes on different parts of an organization, work processes, or individuals
Negotiating/Contracting Skills: organizing, preparing, overseeing, and evaluating work performed by vendors, contingent workers, or outsourcing agents	• Requests for proposals • Written or oral proposals to management or to clients • Written and oral agreements • Management plans for oversight of vendors, contingent workers, or outsourcing agents

Table 5.1: Enabling Outputs Associated with HPI Core Competencies (continued)

Core Competencies	Enabling Outputs
Buy-in/Advocacy Skills: building ownership or support for change among affected individuals, groups, and other stakeholders	• Action plans • Agreements for action • Support for change voiced by performers, performers' managers, process owners, and/or stakeholders
Coping Skills: knowing how to deal with ambiguity and how to handle the stress resulting from change and from multiple meanings or possibilities	• Strategies for managing stress and ambiguity • Strategies for helping others manage stress and ambiguity • Strategies for addressing resistance to change
Ability to See "Big Picture": looking beyond details to see overarching goals and results	• Descriptions of the impact of a human performance improvement strategy on organizational plans, work processes, and individuals
Consulting Skills: understanding the results that stakeholders desire from a process and providing insight into how efficiently and effectively those results can be achieved	• Flow charts • Policy and procedure preparation • Written policies • Written procedures • Preparation of work standards/expectations • Performance contracts

Table 5.2: Outputs Associated with HPI Roles and Competencies

Roles	Competencies	Enabling Outputs	*Terminal Outputs
Analyst—conducts troubleshooting to isolate the cause(s) of human performance gaps or one who identifies areas in which human performance can be improved	Performance Analysis Skills (Front-End Analysis): the process of comparing actual and ideal performance in order to identify performance gaps or opportunities	• Models and plans to guide troubleshooting of human performance gaps • Work plans to guide performance analysis • Information on trends affecting existing or possible future performance gaps • Task analysis • Job analysis	• Persuasive reports to stakeholders about past, present, and future performance gaps and their cause(s)
	Needs Analysis Survey Design and Development Skills (Open-Ended and Structured): preparing written (mail), oral (phone), or electronic (e-mail) surveys using open-ended (essay) and closed (scaled) questions in order to identify human performance improvement needs	• Written (mail) surveys • Oral (phone) surveys • Electronic (e-mail) surveys • Survey administration plans • Research designs • Data analysis and interpretation plans • Reports of needs analysis surveys • Statistical summaries of needs analysis results • Content analysis summaries of needs analysis results	
	Competency Identification Skills: identifying the knowledge and skill requirements of teams, jobs, tasks, roles, and work (McLagan, 1989)	• Work portfolios • Job descriptions • Behavioral events interview guides • Written critical-incident survey questionnaires • Competency models by function, process, organization, or work category • 360-degree assessments	
	Questioning Skills: gathering pertinent information to stimulate insight in individuals and groups through use of interviews and other probing methods (McLagan, 1989)	• Interview guides • Interview administration plans • Content analyses of interview results • Team meeting agendas and plans	

*Terminal outputs are linked directly to a role.

Roles	Competencies	Enabling Outputs	Terminal Outputs
	Analytical Skills (Synthesis): breaking down the components of a larger whole and reassembling them to achieve improved human performance	• Strategies for analyzing the root cause(s) of performance gaps • Fishbone diagrams • Story boards of problem events	
	Work Environment Analytical Skills: examining work environments for issues or characteristics affecting human performance	• Environmental scans • Business/organization plans • Team/group plans • Process improvement strategies/plans	
Intervention Specialist— selects appropriate interventions to address the root cause(s) of performance gaps	**Performance Information Interpretation Skills:** finding useful meaning from the results of performance analysis and helping performers, performers' managers, process owners, and other stakeholders to do so	• Written or oral briefings to performers, performers' managers, process owners, or other stakeholders about the results of performance analysis or cause analysis • Useful information drawn from performance or cause analysis	• Persuasive reports to stakeholders about the appropriate intervention(s) to close past, present, or future performance gap(s)
	Intervention Selection Skills: selecting human performance improvement interventions that address the root cause(s) of performance gaps rather than symptoms or side effects	• Approaches for choosing appropriate human performance improvement strategies to close performance gaps	
	Performance Change Interpretation Skills: forecasting and analyzing the effects of interventions and their consequences	• Written and oral briefings to performers, performers' managers, process owners, and other stakeholders about the likely impact of change or of a human performance improvement intervention on processes, individuals, or the organization • Problem-solving activities to lead performers, performers' managers, process owners, and other stakeholders to discover/forecast the impact of an intervention's implementation on processes, individuals, or the organization	

Roles	Competencies	Enabling Outputs	Terminal Outputs
	Ability to Assess Relationships Among Interventions: examining the effects of multiple human performance improvement interventions on parts of an organization, as well as the effects on the organization's interactions with customers, suppliers, distributors, and workers	• Written and oral briefings to performers, performers' managers, process owners, and other stakeholders about the likely impact of multiple interventions on processes, individuals, or the organization • Problem-solving activities to lead performers, performers' managers, process owners, and other stakeholders to discover/forecast the likely impact of multiple interventions on processes, individuals, or the organization	
	Ability to Identify Critical Business Issues and Changes: determining key business issues and applying that information during the implementation of a human performance improvement intervention	• Organizational analyses • Process analyses • Individual assessments • White papers on human performance improvement strategies • Oral and written briefings to performers, performers' managers, process owners, and stakeholders about possible improvement strategies • Customer satisfaction information/survey results	
	Goal Implementation Skills: ensuring that goals are converted effectively into actions to close existing or pending performance gaps; getting results despite conflicting priorities, lack of resources, or ambiguity	• Written or oral goals for human performance improvement • Performance objectives for interventions • Facilitated performance objectives	

Roles	Competencies	Enabling Outputs	Terminal Outputs
Change Manager—ensures that interventions are implemented in ways consistent with desired results and that they help individuals and groups achieve results	**Change Impetus Skills:** determining what the organization should do to address the cause(s) of a human performance gap at present and in the future	• A convincing case made for the need for change • Organizational sponsorship identified and secured • Evidence of support obtained through commitment of resources • Designs/action plans for introducing and consolidating interventions • Designs/plans for reducing resistance to interventions • Recommendations to management about management's role in introducing and consolidating change • Recommendations to workers about their role in introducing and consolidating change	• Performance improvement interventions effectively monitored with participants and stakeholders • Effective interpersonal interactions among participants and stakeholders of interventions • Tracking systems to compare actual and ideal performance and progress toward narrowing or closing performance gaps, or realizing performance opportunities as the intervention is implemented • Oral and/or written agreements among most or all stakeholders about the results desired from the intervention • Measurable financial or nonfinancial objectives to be achieved during and after implementation of the intervention(s)
	Communication Channel, Informal Network, and Alliance Understanding: knowing how communication moves through an organization by various channels, networks, and alliances; building such channels, networks, and alliances to achieve improvements in productivity and performance	• Communication plans established to keep participants in change and stakeholders of change informed about the progress of the human performance improvement intervention	
	Group Dynamics Process Understanding: understanding how groups function; influencing people so that group, work, and individual needs are addressed (McLagan, 1989)	• Groups successfully observed • Plans for influencing groups based on knowledge of small group development theory	

Roles	Competencies	Enabling Outputs	Terminal Outputs
	Process Consultation Skills: observing individuals and groups for their interactions and the effects of their interactions with others	• Group process observation forms • Descriptions to group members and individuals about the effects of their behavior on a group or on individuals	
	Facilitation Skills: helping performers, performers' managers, process owners, and stakeholders to discover new insights	• Plans for facilitating group discussions • Plans for facilitating individual or group decision making and problem solving	
Evaluator—assesses the impact of interventions and follows up on changes made, actions taken, and results achieved in order to provide participants and stakeholders with information about how well interventions are being implemented	**Performance Gap Evaluation Skills:** measuring or helping others to measure the difference between actual performance and ideal performance	• Human performance improvement evaluation objectives • Human performance improvement evaluation designs and plans • Human performance improvement evaluation instruments • Pre- and post-measures of worker performance • Evaluation findings, conclusions, and recommendations • Reports to management and workers on the outcomes of human performance improvement strategies	• Written and oral reports to participants and stakeholders about the progress of an intervention • Written or oral reports to the organization about performance • Written or oral reports to the organization about progress of interventions • Written or oral reports to work groups or teams about their performance • Written or oral reports to work groups or teams about the progress of interventions • Written or oral reports to management about performance • Written or oral reports to management about interventions

Roles	Competencies	Enabling Outputs	Terminal Outputs
	Ability to Evaluate Results Against Organizational Goals: assessing how well the results of a human performance improvement intervention match intentions	• Linkage of human performance improvement interventions to other change efforts of the organization • Linkage of each human performance improvement intervention with other interventions • Linkage of human performance improvement interventions to organizational plans, goals, and objectives • Linkage of human performance improvement interventions to organizational/business needs	
	Standard Setting Skills: measuring desired results of organizations, processes, or individuals; helping others to establish and measure work expectations	• Work standards/expectations established • Work standards/expectations communicated	
	Ability to Asses Impact on Culture: examining the effects of human performance gaps and human performance improvement interventions on shared beliefs and assumptions about "right" and "wrong" ways of behaving and acting in one organizational setting	• Linkage of human performance improvement interventions to organizational culture	

Roles	Competencies	Enabling Outputs	Terminal Outputs
	Human Performance Improvement Intervention Reviewing Skills: finding ways to evaluate and continuously improve human performance improvement interventions before and during implementation	• Written and oral reports to stakeholders and participants about the progress of an intervention	
	Feedback Skills: collecting information about performance and feeding it back clearly, specifically, and on a timely basis to affected individuals or groups (McLagan, 1989)	• Feedback to the organization about performance • Feedback to the organization about progress of interventions • Feedback to work groups or teams about performance • Feedback to work groups or teams about progress of interventions • Feedback to management about performance • Feedback to management about interventions	

Process for Establishing Measurable Quality Requirements for HPI Work

In *Models for HRD Practice*, McLagan (1989) tied quality requirements to outputs only. In *ASTD Models for Human Performance Improvement*, however, it should be noted that quality requirements may be tied to

- applications of the human performance improvement process model
- demonstrations of single or multiple roles
- demonstrations of competencies
- outputs.

Users of *Models for HRD Practice* have often asked for measurable quality requirements, not just the crite-

ria for measuring quality in HRD work, which are provided in that publication. Such a request assumes, with some naivete, that all organizations and all decision makers possess identical expectations. Unfortunately, that is not always the case. Expectations for performance vary among organizations and among stakeholders and decision makers. Hence, measuring quality and evaluating the performance of those doing human performance work is positioned in the center of the circle shown in Figure 5.2. Quality exists in the mind of the beholder—and the beholders may vary.

When developing a process to formulate and use quality requirements for human performance improvement work, many decisions must be made

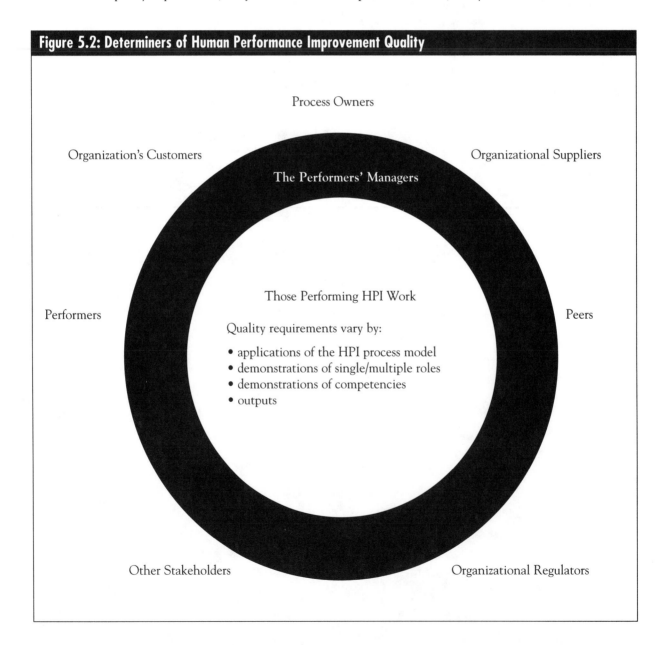

Figure 5.2: Determiners of Human Performance Improvement Quality

Process Owners

Organization's Customers

Organizational Suppliers

The Performers' Managers

Performers

Peers

Those Performing HPI Work

Quality requirements vary by:

- applications of the HPI process model
- demonstrations of single/multiple roles
- demonstrations of competencies
- outputs

Other Stakeholders

Organizational Regulators

before a clear direction can be established. These important decisions are depicted schematically in Figure 5.3.

Those who do HPI work, along with decision makers and stakeholders, need to decide what limitations, if any, may affect the choice of quality requirements that are formulated and implemented for such work. For example, do those performing human performance improvement work have a free hand in establishing quality requirements unique to what they do? Or must quality requirements comply with organizationally established quality requirements expressed in job descriptions, union agreements, organizational performance evaluation forms, or externally imposed requirements?

Those involved in HPI work also must decide whether the human performance improvement inter-

vention is to be evaluated on its own or only as a result of the success or failure of what it does (e.g., specific projects or HPI interventions). Decide why the quality requirements are being established. Is the aim to appraise performance; develop individuals, teams, or groups; provide timely, concrete, and specific feedback to individuals and/or groups; or serve some other purpose or combination of purposes?

Decide what quality requirements are to be established, including any or all of the following:

- applications of the HPI process model
- demonstrations of single or multiple roles
- demonstrations of competencies
- outputs.

Decide who will be involved in establishing the quality requirements for human performance improvement

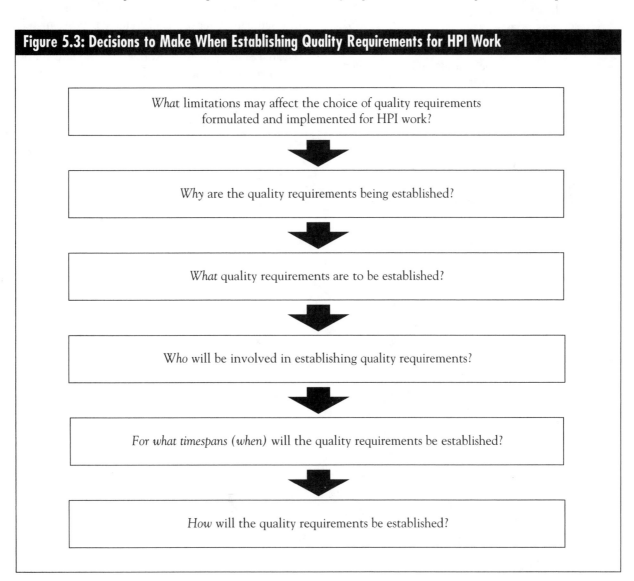

Figure 5.3: Decisions to Make When Establishing Quality Requirements for HPI Work

What limitations may affect the choice of quality requirements formulated and implemented for HPI work?

Why are the quality requirements being established?

What quality requirements are to be established?

Who will be involved in establishing quality requirements?

For what timespans (when) will the quality requirements be established?

How will the quality requirements be established?

work. Will it include only some—or all—of the various stakeholders of an intervention?

Decide for what time span (when) the quality requirements will be established. Are the quality requirements meant to be continuing, fixed in time, or future-oriented?

Decide for what location(s) (where) the quality requirements will be established. Are the quality requirements meant to be

◆ function-specific (tied to HPI work in a particular area of the organization or unique to one occupation)
◆ culture-specific (tied to HPI work in a particular geographical area)
◆ situation-specific (tied to one project or intervention)
◆ some combination of any or all of the above?

Decide how the quality requirements will be established. Will they be

◆ established by the organization's management and imposed on those performing HPI work
◆ formulated by those performing HPI work and/or by the organization's management and then negotiated until all stakeholders have found them to be acceptable

◆ established and used by those performing HPI work only
◆ formulated and used in some other way?

Various approaches may be used, of course, to establish quality requirements for human performance improvement work once these decisions have been made. For instance, it is possible to use each step in the HPI process model as a basis for identifying the most likely, or most desirable, behaviors that are exhibited by those who perform HPI work and then establish measurable quality requirements by polling exemplary performers and/or other stakeholders for each behavior.

The Author

William J. Rothwell is professor of human resource development in the Department of Adult Education, Instructional Systems, and Workforce Education and Development at the University Park campus of Pennsylvania State University. Rothwell is also director of the Institute for Research in Training and Development at Penn State.

Human resource development professionals are in a unique position to influence ethical awareness in the workplace. Even a basic understanding of ethical theory can give these professionals the information they need to recognize the ethical implications of their interventions.

Those who do human performance improvement work must be able to assess and analyze the organization's performance requirements effectively. Over time, many experts have made this observation. Among them: Harless in 1973, Gilbert in 1978, Mager and Pipe in 1984, Kaufman in 1986, Rossett in 1987, Rummler and Brache in 1990, Swanson in 1994, Dean in 1994, and Langdon in 1995. But in 1988, A. Bednar observed in *Performance Improvement Quarterly* that practitioners also have a duty to ensure that changes resulting from HR interventions are in line with organizational goals. That same year, Odin Westgaard wrote in *A Credo for Performance Technologists* that practitioners also have a duty to use their skills to support humane, socially responsible, life-fulfilling ends.

Still some misconceptions exist about the ethical aspect of human performance improvement work. Some say that because a professional who does HPI work takes on the role of objective researcher in verifying results of a process, the output of that process—and the professional's related decisions and actions—must necessarily be ethical. But without knowledge of factors that influence ethical behavior and ethical decision making, even seasoned professionals may fail to recognize and address ethical concerns.

The key to influencing the ethical environment of an organization while helping to improve performance and increase productivity and profits is this: People who do human performance improvement work must possess a sound knowledge of ethics and must take responsibility for both the intervention processes they use and the results they achieve.

Professional Expectations

Under unethical behavior, the *credo* specifies that professionals involved in human performance improvement work should not

- violate professional, academic, or business ethics with such less-than-honest billing practices as submitting low bids, but higher final bills
- promise that solutions will work when they may not
- make false claims regarding return on investment
- use client information for personal gain
- falsify data
- compromise human performance improvement for personal or political gain by providing interventions that are acceptable to the client but ill-suited to the context
- take credit for another person's work
- make false claims about another's behaviors or potential accomplishments.

In explaining the need for these caveats, Westgaard observed that:

> The basic value which identifies true professionals is their drive to give full measure and do their best. To do less, to settle for a half-measure, is disrespectful of oneself, others, and the profession. Failure to establish ethical controls results in unfair competition, misunderstandings with clients, and risks of scandals to the profession.

He added that those who do human performance improvement work "must seek to lessen the possibility of unfair competitive practices by establishing and adhering to ethical guidelines."

Clients' Advantage

Here's another compelling reason for practitioners to expand their knowledge of ethics: Being aware of ethics enables professionals to help clients achieve their goals in ethical ways.

Every member of an organization should be aware that the ethical climate is one of the factors that can damage employee motivation, which ultimately may affect performance and productivity. Examples of such negative influences include

- inconsistent application of policies
- lack of concern for employees' rights and safety
- the organization's failure to comply with laws
- misrepresentation to suppliers or clients
- withholding information or establishing unrealistic expectations to gain control or power.

Creating a sound ethical climate can contribute to the effectiveness of human performance improvement efforts. As practitioners engage in the various tasks (e.g., conducting a performance analysis or cause analysis, selecting or implementing an intervention, or evaluating the impact of an intervention), they seldom work with just one level of the organization. Different ethical viewpoints exist at different organizational levels. The varying degrees of cooperation, amounts of information, and commitment to follow up on solutions at each level also have significant effects on any results.

Often those who do HPI work struggle to overcome these differences. But if they work from the premise that creating and maintaining an ethical environment is both within the mission of an effective organization and good business practice, then they'll have a context for addressing ethical problems in a straightforward manner. They'll be able to suggest the need to examine the ethical agreement of different functions, policies, and organizational levels to ensure an environment that encourages top performance.

They'll also be able to fulfill one of their ethical responsibilities as human performance improvement professionals; that of helping the organization recognize how a solution implemented at one level can affect the entire organization. This also helps decision makers at various levels to become aware of how their decisions have significant impact throughout the organization. (See Table 6.1, opposite.)

Performance Improvement Professionals and the Corporate Ethicist

Corporate ethicists should be concerned whenever there is actual or potential harm—whether physical, mental, or economic—to any individual or group within the organization. They also should be concerned when the rights of one individual compete with another or when the rights of different organizational levels compete with each other. Cooke (Dean, 1993) focused on such situations by raising the following questions:

◆ Is the behavior or anticipated behavior arbitrary or capricious?

◆ Does it unfairly single out any individual or group?

◆ Does it violate moral and legal rights of any individual or group?

◆ Does it conform to accepted ethical and moral standards?

◆ Are there alternative courses of action that are less likely to cause harm?

In 1989, Patricia McLagan wrote in the *Journal of Management Studies* that human performance improvement professionals should be aware of such key ethical issues as confidentiality, inappropriate requests, intellectual property, truth in claims, organizational versus individual needs, customer and user participation, conflicts of interest, personal biases, individual and population differences, appropriate interventions, intervention consequences, fair pricing, and use of power. Human performance improvement professionals and ethicists can help managers tend to these issues, especially when they involve the consequences of a manager's decisions.

Rather than attend to the quality of activities, behaviors, and processes of decision making, managers are often trained to look at the data collected and the consequences of an outcome. This approach may fail to provide an ethical climate because it stems from an ends-justify-the-means logic, known as consequential, utilitarian, or goal-oriented management (Krupp, 1961; Pfeffer, 1978; Keely, 1979). Managers who use this goal-oriented approach may be less likely to consider the ethics of the means used to arrive at decisions or outcomes.

Applications of Ethical Knowledge

The actual process of making ethical decisions or helping managers make them is seldom as easy as simply selecting the right choice. Although the right choice is sometimes obvious, often a manager must choose between two alternatives that are both right.

In this situation it's helpful to apply a step-by-step decision-making process. According to the *Business Ethics Study Guide*, published in 1988 by the Aresty Institute of Executive Education at the University of Pennsylvania's Wharton School of Business, when there are two right choices, ethical decisions depend on both the decision-making process and the experience, intelligence, and integrity of the decision maker. In many instances, training and coaching can both enhance the decision-making process and enrich the experience of the decision maker (Dean, 1993).

Models of ethical decision making help guide managers through ethical issues. In *Business and Its Environment*, Baron (1991) says that models "present ethical systems and methods of reasoning that deepen one's understanding of a situation, identify relevant moral concerns, and provide a means of evaluating actions and policies."

Most models contain the same basic ideas featured in Werhane's seven-step process for ethical decision making (1992). This process is especially helpful for those who do human performance improvement work because it provides an entry point for needs assessment and can reveal aspects of problems early in the process, which may boost the effectiveness and efficiency of the needs assessment. The seven steps are as follows (Werhane, 1992):

1. **Identify relevant facts.** These are key factors that shape the situation and influence ethical issues.

2. **Define ethical issues.** Note all issues related to the situation, and separate ethical from nonethical issues. Identify issues at all organizational levels.

3. **Identify the primary stakeholders.** Be able to name those individuals and groups involved in the situation that will be affected by a decision, and consider how the decision will affect them.

4. **Determine all alternative interventions.**

Table 6.1: Summary of Ethical Issues Affecting the Roles of Those Doing HPI Work

Ethical Issues	Roles			
Those doing human performance work encounter such ethical issues as...	Analyst	Intervention Specialist	Change Manager	Evaluator
Maintaining an objective stance when examining and verifying the results of a process	✔	✔	✔	✔
Taking responsibility for the impact of their work on other people	✔	✔	✔	✔
Maintaining professional, academic, and business ethics by ensuring that final bills match original work bids	✔	✔	✔	✔
Making realistic claims to clients about the impact of human performance improvement interventions or strategies	✔	✔	✔	✔
Making realistic claims about the return on investment of interventions	✔	✔	✔	✔
Maintaining client confidentiality, using information only to help the client and not for personal gain	✔	✔	✔	✔
Ensuring that data are accurate, reliable, and valid and are never falsified	✔	✔	✔	✔
Preserving the integrity of human performance improvement work by matching human performance improvement interventions provided to client context and need	✔	✔	✔	✔
Taking credit for one's own work only	✔	✔	✔	✔
Providing accurate information about the behaviors or potential accomplishments of other people—and avoiding false claims about the behaviors or accomplishments of others	✔	✔	✔	✔
Encouraging and modeling consistent application of policies	✔	✔	✔	✔
Preserving employee rights and safety	✔	✔	✔	✔
Maintaining compliance with applicable laws, rules, and regulations	✔	✔	✔	✔
Accurately representing oneself and one's human performance improvement intervention processes and results	✔	✔	✔	✔
Providing adequate information to other people	✔	✔	✔	✔

Note: Items in the left column of the table are adapted from A credo for performance technologists. *Westgaard, O. (1988). Reprinted with permission from the International Society for Performance Improvement.*

5. **List ethical implications of each alternative.** Evaluate each according to both the impact on stakeholders and on the ethical theories.

6. **List practical constraints.** Identify any factors that might limit the implementation of alternatives or make implementation too difficult or risky.

7. **Determine what action to take.** Review the information in the preceding steps, select an action, and identify an implementation strategy.

Ethics Programs

Training courses in ethics are valuable, but they may not be sufficient to redress ethical wrongs or to demonstrate concern for ethical issues. Simply stated, training will not solve problems if the organization doesn't support ethical decision making. Through a careful performance analysis, those who do HPI work can help their clients determine whether training is the appropriate approach for improving both the ethical climate and the decision-making process. To identify the proper solution, the human performance improvement professional must be aware of the factors that contribute to an ethically sound environment (Dean, 1993, 1994).

In *Ethics Effectiveness Quick-Test*, F. Navran (1990) refers to needs assessments as ethics audits. He found that ethical effectiveness is achieved when an organization designs, develops, and implements such elements as

- clear organizational values that provide direction and consistency in decision making
- ethics strategies that define goals and objectives and allow the organization to measure progress
- ethics policies and procedures that describe ways to implement ethics strategies
- measures of ethical effectiveness that determine if ethical standards are being maintained and if the standards are yielding the desired results
- rewards for ethical behaviors and decisions that the organization wants to sustain
- guidelines for ethical decision making that offer directions to decision makers who must deal with situations not addressed in policies and procedures
- assessment of ethical climate to determine common ground between general perceptions of the organization's and the individual's values
- support for ethical practices from formal and informal systems and application of ethical guidelines to all jobs
- ethical leadership practices that model the ethical behavior expected of all employees
- evaluation of the impact of ethical practices on productivity and profitability

- ethics education and training to enable employees to act on their responsibilities
- respect for employees' personal values that encourages their support for the work the organization expects of them.

Looking Toward the Future

Ethical standards for those who do human performance improvement work should come from the HR profession. Such standards for their client organizations should come from the workplace itself, and those who do HPI work can help their clients develop those standards. To do this, those who do human performance improvement work should invest time in learning about the research and theory that define business ethics. The next step is to design and develop refined ethical heuristics that are based on the best literature in the field and the most reliable studies by subject matter experts and ethicists. Finally, those who do HPI work must use and model these ethics standards as they practice their craft.

The Author

Peter J. Dean, II, is currently a senior fellow, The Wharton Ethics Program, Department of Legal Studies, The Wharton School at The University of Pennsylvania, and a tenured, associate professor, Physician Executive MBA Program at The University of Tennessee. He has been an assistant professor of management and organization in the Smeal College of Business Administration at Penn State University, and an assistant professor and regional coordinator of instructional systems (training design and development) at Penn State. Dean received his Ph.D. and subsequently taught at The University of Iowa. He was the recipient of the 1993 Excellence in Teaching Award at Penn State University at Great Valley, and the 1995 MBA Core Curriculum Cluster Teaching Award at The Wharton School. He has published in *The Journal of Business Ethics, Human Resource Development Quarterly, Performance Improvement Quarterly, Performance Improvement Journal*, and *The Australian Journal of Educational Technology*. He is the current Editor of *Performance Improvement Quarterly*. He has edited *Performance Engineering at Work*, co-authored an instructional manual for *Managing Business Ethics*, co-edited five books on Performance Improvement Models, Methods and Measures, and co-edited *The Business of Medicine: What Every Physician Leader Needs to Know*. He has consulted for numerous international companies and lectured in Switzerland, India, Pakistan, Sri Lanka, Norway, Australia, Germany, and Canada.

This section describes the intended audiences and uses for *ASTD Models for Human Performance Improvement.*

HRD Practitioner Uses

HRD practitioners form one possible user group for this book. Some of the ways they can use the study are described below.

Designing jobs, work, or tasks. This book can serve as a useful tool to help HRD practitioners make the transition from training and development, organization development, or career development specialist to human performance improvement generalist. A key advantage to making such a transition is that HRD practitioners who choose this path are no longer limited to offering training as the only solution for performance problems.

Identifying or clarifying work expectations and competency levels. For HRD practitioners who do wish to make a transition from traditional training into human performance improvement, this book suggests a place to begin when identifying what they should be doing in this new role. It also describes how to assess, through various tools, their current competence level in the HPI process.

Managing projects. The HPI process model can be a flexible blueprint for organizing projects. This book can be useful when organizing and managing project plans to improve human performance.

Prompting feedback on performance. Improving the feedback performers receive can be one of the most powerful interventions. This applies to people who do HPI work as much as to any worker. By using the roles, competencies, and outputs described here as a reference point, people who do HPI work have the basis for soliciting specific, concrete, and timely feedback from customers and other stakeholders about their performance. This can lead to continuous improvement in their own performance.

Planning their careers. Training and development traditionally has led to career paths in human resources management. But when HRD practitioners undertake HPI work, they begin to prepare themselves for careers in human resource management and line management. The reason: The roles, competencies, and outputs of human resource management and line management merge in those of HPI work.

Identifying professional development needs. In what areas do HRD practitioners need to be developed? Using this book, HRD practitioners can examine their professional development needs to identify areas in which they may need to increase or deepen their knowledge.

Documenting accomplishments. This book provides the basis for a common language across organizations. By documenting work accomplishments in terms of the roles, competencies, and outputs described here, HRD practitioners can show what they have accomplished. This can be helpful in moving across organizations. Such a common language is particularly important as organizations become more flexible in their staffing arrangements and as HRD practitioners shift their expectations from lifelong careers with one or a few employers to stints in different jobs and organizations.

Training others. In the true spirit of empowerment and involvement, HRD practitioners work to build the capacity of others—including their co-workers, line managers, and employees—around the HPI process model. This book can be a starting point for developing training programs on human performance improvement. More specifically, it can be a framework for analyzing training needs linked to HPI and for designing, developing, and delivering training programs around those needs.

Consulting with others. When HRD practitioners undertake new roles as performance consultants who work with others to achieve improved performance, they must go beyond training to adopt a new focus for their work. The HPI process model provides a useful and flexible blueprint to guide consulting engagements, whether carried out by internal HRD practitioners working with employees and managers or by external HRD consultants called in from outside organizations.

Preparing for the future. By referring to the future trends identified in this book, people who do HPI work can prepare themselves for the future. Clearly the HRD field is headed toward increasingly emphasizing results (improved performance), rather than such activities as training. By considering the trends affecting the workforce and examining how they may affect HPI roles, competencies, and outputs, people who do HPI work can deal with the so-called moving target effect in which unfolding trends change desired results even as actions are underway to achieve the desired results.

Maintaining ethical standards. Maintaining ethical standards is important because some critics of HPI claim that too much emphasis on performance dehumanizes people and minimizes the importance of balancing individual and organizational needs. This does not have to be true. People who do HPI work can be as sensitive to individual needs as they are to organizational results. This book provides one means to do this.

HRD Manager Uses

HRD managers oversee a staff of HRD practitioners or bear authority for an HRD department without a staff. Those who function as HRD managers include training directors, human resource managers, HRD consultants who hire subcontractors, HRD practitioners who are positioned inside one organizational division to coordinate HRD efforts, and others bearing important responsibilities for the oversight of HRD work. HRD managers will find the *ASTD Models* useful in helping them to meet their responsibilities and to fulfill the following functions.

Reinventing the role of the training department. Many organizations are taking stock of what they expect from a training department. As they do so, many organizations are reinventing the training department to focus on improving human performance. But, transitioning from a traditional training function to a human performance improvement function is a major change effort that requires careful planning, clear goals and expectations, a continuing effort to implement the change, involvement by key stakeholders, and continuous evaluation.

The *ASTD Models* can offer a vision of what a reinvented training department should be doing and what reinvented trainers should be doing. It can thus be a starting point for reinventing the traditional training department for HRD managers who are inclined to build an impetus for this change.

Planning for staff and staff development. What types of individuals are needed to do human performance improvement work? The *ASTD Models* provides valuable information that can help answer this question. Indeed, the *ASTD Models* provides a starting point for

◆ assessing the competency levels of existing HRD staff, line managers, and others who can play a part in human performance improvement
◆ managing outsourcing opportunities
◆ hiring vendors to assist with any facet of the HPI process model
◆ identifying or clarifying work expectations for those who do HPI work
◆ designing jobs, work, or tasks for those who do HPI work
◆ overseeing HPI projects or interventions
◆ providing feedback on performance to those who do HPI work
◆ offering advice and consultation about career planning for people who do HPI work
◆ identifying the professional development needs of people who do HPI work

◆ documenting the accomplishments of people who do HPI work
◆ training people to apply the HPI process model.

Preparing for the future. HRD managers bear responsibility for setting a direction for their departments or functions. The trends identified in the *ASTD Models* provide a starting point for thinking about ways that HPI work can be positioned to anticipate or react to those trends.

Maintaining ethical standards. HRD managers should establish a moral climate where people can do HPI work. The *ASTD Models* provides a tool for examining ethical issues, crafting codes of conduct for people who do human performance improvement work, holding individuals accountable to those standards, and troubleshooting ethical dilemmas as they arise.

Line Manager Uses

Line managers bear primary responsibility for serving customers, making products, dealing with suppliers, and meeting distributor needs. Most people in organizations report to line managers. In manufacturing firms, line managers are positioned around the manufacturing process. In service firms, line managers are positioned around direct service delivery. They are distinct from staff managers, who support line managers.

Line managers also bear primary responsibility for troubleshooting or anticipating human performance gaps, formulating HPI interventions, selecting appropriate interventions, managing change, and evaluating change efforts. They can receive advice on these issues, or line managers can become HPI workers themselves. The *ASTD Models* provides a useful tool for line managers who wish to apply the HPI process model.

Interacting effectively with the training, HRD, or human performance improvement department. How can the HRD or HPI function help line managers? The *ASTD Models* provides a common language by which to facilitate communication across line and staff units. By referring to steps in the HPI process model and the roles, competencies, and outputs of HPI work, line and staff managers can share a common language.

Analyzing performance. The *ASTD Models* offers a simple model for troubleshooting performance problems or for planning improved performance. When line managers become familiar with these models, they can become their own consultants.

Choosing interventions, managing change, and evaluating results. The *ASTD Models* suggests many possible causes of past, present, or future human performance gaps and identifies many possible interventions.

By becoming an expert at using the HPI process model, line managers may learn to choose appropriate interventions, manage change, and evaluate results.

Employee Uses

Empowered and involved workers are willing and able to analyze human performance gaps, choose appropriate human performance improvement interventions, implement the interventions, and evaluate results. The *ASTD Models* provides guidelines for this process. All employees—not just specialists or HRD practitioners—bear these responsibilities.

Academician Uses

Many undergraduate and graduate HRD programs exist in the United States and in other nations. Some are offered for degrees and some are offered for continuing education credit. Administrators, faculty, and staff working in those programs can use the *ASTD Models* as a framework for assessing program needs, planning program enhancements and courses, assessing learners, formulating and implementing research agenda, advising learners enrolled in the programs (or considering enrollment), developing faculty, and evaluating program processes and outcomes.

Assessing needs. What are the needs of learners and employers for people who do human performance improvement? The *ASTD Models* provides a framework for conducting academic program needs assessments in order to

◆ assess employers' needs for people who are able to apply the HPI process model

◆ assess interests in academic course work on HPI among prospective students.

Planning programs and courses. The *ASTD Models* provides a framework for

◆ establishing new courses or revising old courses based on the HPI process model, the roles described by it, the competencies stemming from it, future trends listed in it, and ethical issues identified by it

◆ benchmarking programs or courses against offerings at other academic institutions.

Assessing learners. The *ASTD Models* provides a framework for

◆ identifying sources of prospective students based on the people who perform HPI work

◆ assessing differences between individual student competencies and the competencies required for success in HPI work, which can become the basis for individualized learning plans or individualized plans of study.

Formulating and implementing a research agenda. A research agenda is, of course, a long-range plan to guide research. Since *ASTD Models* was based on an exploratory study and is intended to be an evolving process, it furnishes the basis for additional research. After all, not all important questions about HPI work have been answered here. The following questions warrant further investigation.

◆ How do the roles, competencies, outputs, ethical issues, and future trends identified by this study match up to the expectations of various groups that traditionally have been key stakeholders for HRD practitioners (e.g., CEOs, senior executives, middle managers, and customers)?

◆ What similarities and differences exist between applications of the HPI process model in the United States and in other nations or cultures?

◆ How does emerging technology affect the roles, competencies, and outputs of HPI work?

Advising learners. Students enrolled in academic programs in HRD or HPI often have individualized needs for advice about what courses to take, what career goals to pursue, and how to build the competencies they need to realize their career goals. The *ASTD Models* is a useful tool for organizing such discussions. By using it, faculty and students can ensure that they are using common terminology.

Managing and developing faculty. Faculty members who teach in academic programs in HRD or human performance improvement must stay current if they are to teach effectively and provide appropriate guidance to students. Just as the *ASTD Models* is a useful tool for assessing individual student competencies and developing student plans of study, it also can be useful for assessing faculty competencies and suggesting professional development activities to build those competencies.

Evaluating program processes and results. Accountability is the key word for the 1990s. Just as HRD practitioners are under increasing pressure to demonstrate that their efforts lead to payoffs for their learners and their organizations, so too are academic programs under pressure to demonstrate that they are delivering effective results. The *ASTD Models* is a standard against which to evaluate academic program processes and results. External review teams called in to colleges and universities to audit instructional processes and outcomes of academic HRD or HPI programs may rely on the *ASTD Models* as a benchmark against which to assess what competencies students should be building and what outputs students should be capable of producing when finished with their programs.

The Author

William J. Rothwell is professor of human resource development in the Department of Adult Education, Instructional Systems, and Workforce Education and Development at the University Park campus of Pennsylvania State University. Rothwell is also director of the Institute for Research in Training and Development at Penn State.

▲ SECTION 8 CONCLUSION

Developing human resources remains an important function of organizations. Through training and development, organization development, and career development, individuals and groups are made more productive and are prepared for present and future challenges. Development also helps ensure organizational continuity by providing successors for people in all parts of organizations.

However, organizational stakeholders and decision makers increasingly are looking for ways to see improved human performance through methods that transcend development. While not diminishing the importance of development, that means that trainers, HRD practitioners, managers, and others having a role in development should increase their repertoire of competencies and begin applying human performance improvement.

ASTD Models for Human Performance Improvement is intended to serve as a guide to human performance improvement practice for trainers, HRD practitioners, managers, college professors, and others who do HPI work. It provides ideas and suggestions to support them as they undertake the daunting challenges they face in the future. It is meant to stimulate dialogue and further study about the many ways that human performance may be improved.

The Author

William J. Rothwell is professor of human resource development in the Department of Adult Education, Instructional Systems, and Workforce Education and Development at the University Park campus of Pennsylvania State University. Rothwell is also director of the Institute for Research in Training and Development at Penn State.

SECTION 9   Assessment Tools
By William J. Rothwell and Ethan S. Sanders

We hope that the preceding pages have given you a better understanding of the competencies for human performance improvement work. In order to help you apply this new knowledge to your own circumstances, we have developed several assessment tools. This section includes the following inventories:

Worksheet 1:   Reviewer Selection Form

Worksheet 2:   Profile of Enabling Outputs Associated with HPI Core Competencies

Worksheet 3:   Self-Assessment Inventory

Worksheet 4:   360°-Assessment Inventory

Worksheet 5:   Summary of Results

Worksheet 6:   Development Planning Tool

Worksheet 7:   Learning Contract

Worksheet 8:   Preparation for the Future

Worksheet 9:   Resolving Ethical Dilemmas

These inventories can be used to gather a 360-degree assessment of your strengths and development needs in relation to HPI work. They also help you to understand which competencies are important to develop for your current work situation and which competencies will become increasingly important in the future. Once you have this information, worksheet 6 will help you to brainstorm ways of filling your knowledge gaps, and worksheet 7 will help you to formalize your development objectives into a learning contract.

By following the directions at the top of each worksheet, you can complete this process in a few hours.

Purpose of this self-assessment.

Before you begin the assessment process, it is important to have a clear idea of what you are hoping to accomplish.

Which of the following reasons best describes your purpose for wanting to complete a competency review process? Answering this question is important because your reason(s) will affect what you need from the assessment process and how you should interpret the results. Place a check in all of the appropriate boxes below. You may want to rank your answers, starting with "1" as your primary reason, "2" as your secondary reason, and so on.

❏ To benchmark myself against the competencies described in this book.

❏ To move into a new role that involves a great amount of HPI responsibility.

❏ To document my current competency level.

❏ To determine how HPI will change my current job in the foreseeable future.

❏ To benchmark my current skills against those of other training professionals.

❏ To use as a supplement to my performance review.

❏ Other: _____

Identifying reviewers.

Given your reason(s) for entering this review process, consider which individuals within your organization would best be able to assess your present competency level objectively. It is also possible to select people who are not within your organization, but they must be familiar with your work. It is important that you select several (two or three) of your peers, and if you manage people, several of your direct reports. If you do not have any direct reports, consider people in other departments whom you interact with daily. Also, in order to gain a well-rounded perspective, you need to involve your direct supervisor in this process. Please list all of your potential candidates in the spaces provided on the following pages.

Worksheet 1: Reviewer Selection Form

Peers:

1. Name: _____

    Job Title and Work Function: _____

    _____

    _____

    _____

    Why will this person provide helpful information? _____

    _____

    _____

    _____

2. Name: _____

    Job Title and Work Function: _____

    _____

    _____

    _____

    Why will this person provide helpful information? _____

    _____

    _____

    _____

3. Name: _____

    Job Title and Work Function: _____

    _____

    _____

    _____

    Why will this person provide helpful information? _____

    _____

    _____

    _____

This worksheet is reproducible.

Direct Reports:

1. Name: _____

    Job Title and Work Function: _____

    _____

    _____

    _____

    Why will this person provide helpful information? _____

    _____

    _____

    _____

    _____

2. Name: _____

    Job Title and Work Function: _____

    _____

    _____

    _____

    Why will this person provide helpful information? _____

    _____

    _____

    _____

3. Name: _____

    Job Title and Work Function: _____

    _____

    _____

    _____

    Why will this person provide helpful information? _____

    _____

    _____

    _____

This worksheet is reproducible.

Supervisor:

1. Name: _Debbie Meyer_

   Job Title and Work Function: _Performance Improvement Dept. Head_

   _____

   _____

   _____

Why will this person provide helpful information?

To guide me in personal performance improvement

To share resources she has used that I may
not be aware of.

To improve the performance of the department.

_____

_____

_____

_____

_____

This worksheet is reproducible.

Profile of your current and future work.

The following worksheet lists key human performance improvement outputs or deliverables resulting from HPI work. Check up to 12 outputs that are most important to your work now, as well as those that will be most important 3 to 5 years from now. Add outputs if more are necessary to reflect the full extent of your work, but check no more than 12 outputs for current and 12 outputs for future work from the entire list of 158 outputs.

The resulting picture of your current and future work will serve as the basis for prioritizing your competency development needs. Please note that although the outputs are grouped by roles, your work may involve outputs in one, a few, or many roles. Also realize that the outputs and competencies represent the full range of human performance improvement work, so you are not expected to have or develop expertise in all the areas listed.

Worksheet 2: Profile of Enabling Outputs Associated with HPI Core Competencies

Core Competencies of Human Performance Improvement Work/Outputs	Current Work	Future Work
Core Competency: Industry Awareness 1. Descriptions of industry/organizational status	☒	☒
Core Competency: Leadership Skills 2. Positive influence on others exhibited	☒	☒
Core Competency: Interpersonal Relationship Skills 3. Positive relationships established and maintained with clients, stakeholders, and decision makers	☒	☒
Core Competency: Technological Awareness and Understanding 4. Facility in using technology	☒	☒
5. Criteria for choosing optimal or cost-effective technology	☐	☒
6. Selection of appropriate technology	☒	☒
7. Designs for establishing, implementing, or evaluating performance support systems	☐	☒
8. Designs for integrating the work that people do and the technology that people use to achieve desired results	☐	☒
9. Environmental scans for appropriate technology	☒	☒
Core Competency: Problem-Solving Skills 10. Strategies for groups, teams, or individuals to discover, present, or anticipate performance gaps	☒	☒
11. Application of quality tools to identify special and general causes of problems (histograms, trend charts, etc.)	☐	☒
12. Written and oral briefings to performers, performers' managers, process owners, and other stakeholders about performance gaps	☐	☒

This worksheet is reproducible.

Core Competencies of Human Performance Improvement Work/Outputs	Current Work	Future Work
13. Problem-solving activities to lead performers, performers' managers, process owners, and other stakeholders to discover/forecast the likely impact of multiple interventions on processes, individuals, or the organization	☐	☒
Core Competency: Systems Thinking and Understanding 14. Systems flow charts showing the impact of interventions on processes, individuals, or the organization	☒	☒
Core Competency: Performance Understanding 15. Written and oral descriptions of performance	☐	☒
16. Visual charts, process descriptions, or other aids to show performance	☐	☒
Core Competency: Knowledge of Interventions 17. Plans for employee recruitment or selection programs	☒	☒
18. Plans for employee orientation programs	☒	☒
19. Plans for employee training programs using systematic approaches	☒	☒
20. Plans for establishing learning organizations	☒	☒
21. Plans for employee performance appraisal practices and programs	☐	☒
22. Plans for career development programs	☒	☒
23. Plans for organization development interventions	☐	☒
24. Plans for compensation, reward, and incentive programs	☐	☒
25. Plans for employee feedback programs	☐	☒
26. Plans for employee discipline programs	☐	☒
27. Plans for employee counseling and wellness programs	☐	☐
28. Plans for safety programs	☒	☒
29. Plans for improved tools and equipment	☐	☐
30. Plans for improved on-the-job training	☒	☒
31. Plans for improved on-the-job learning	☒	☒
32. Plans for job aids	☒	☒
33. Plans for organizational design	☐	☒
34. Plans for job design	☐	☒

This worksheet is reproducible.

Core Competencies of Human Performance Improvement Work/Outputs	Current Work	Future Work
35. Plans for task design	☒	☒
36. Plans for ergonomic improvements	☐	☒
37. Plans for improved employee staff planning and forecasting programs	☐	☒
38. Plans for other human performance improvement strategies/interventions including the following:	☐	☒
Core Competency: Business Understanding 39. Flow charts of work processes	☒	☒
40. Flow charts of organizational operations/networks	☒	☒
41. Flow charts of interactions with customers and other stakeholders	☒	☒
42. Cash flow statements	☐	☒
43. Budget documents	☐	☒
44. Income sheets and balance statements	☐	☒
Core Competency: Organization Understanding 45. Stories about organizational culture/history and experiences	☒	☒
46. Descriptions of the likely impact of changes on different parts of an organization, work processes, or individuals	☒	☒
Core Competency: Negotiating/Contracting Skills 47. Requests for proposals	☐	☒
48. Written or oral proposals to management or to clients	☒	☒
49. Written and oral agreements	☐	☒
50. Management plans for oversight of vendors, contingent workers, or outsourcing agents	☒	☒
Core Competency: Buy-in/Advocacy Skills 51. Action plans	☒	☒
52. Agreements for action	☐	☒
53. Support for change voiced by performers, performers' managers, process owners, and/or stakeholders	☐	☒
Core Competency: Coping Skills 54. Strategies for managing stress and ambiguity	☒	☒
55. Strategies for helping others manage stress and ambiguity	☒	☒

This worksheet is reproducible.

Core Competencies of Human Performance Improvement Work/Outputs	Current Work	Future Work
56. Strategies for addressing resistance to change	☒	☒
Core Competency: Ability to See "Big Picture" 57. Descriptions of the impact of a human performance improvement strategy on organizational plans, work processes, and individuals	☒	☒
Core Competency: Consulting Skills 58. Flow charts	☒	☒
59. Policy and procedure preparation	☒	☒
60. Written policies	☒	☒
61. Written procedures	☒	☒
62. Preparation of work standards/expectations	☒	☒
63. Performance contracts	☐	☒
Enabling and Terminal Outputs Associated with HPI Roles		
Analyst: Enabling Outputs 64. Models and plans to guide troubleshooting of human performance gaps	☐	☒
65. Work plans to guide performance analysis	☐	☒
66. Information on trends affecting existing or possible future performance gaps	☐	☒
67. Task analysis	☒	☒
68. Job analysis	☒	☒
69. Written (mail) surveys	☐	☐
70. Oral (phone) surveys	☐	☐
71. Electronic (e-mail) surveys	☒	☒
72. Survey administration plans	☐	☒
73. Research designs	☐	☒
74. Data analysis and interpretation plans	☐	☒
75. Reports of needs analysis surveys	☐	☒
76. Statistical summaries of needs analysis results	☐	☒

This worksheet is reproducible.

Enabling and Terminal Outputs Associated with HPI Roles	Current Work	Future Work
77. Content analysis summaries of needs analysis results	☐	☒
78. Work portfolios	☒	☒
79. Job descriptions	☒	☒
80. Behavioral events interview guides	☐	☒
81. Written critical-incident survey questionnaires	☐	☒
82. Competency models by function, process, organization, or work category	☒	☒
83. 360-degree assessments	☒	☒
84. Interview guides	☒	☒
85. Interview administration plans	☒	☒
86. Content analyses of interview results	☒	☒
87. Team meeting agendas and plans	☒	☒
88. Strategies for analyzing the root cause(s) of performance gaps	☐	☒
89. Fishbone diagrams	☐	☒
90. Story boards of problem events	☐	☒
91. Environmental scans	☐	☒
92. Business/organization plans	☒	☒
93. Team/group plans	☒	☒
94. Process improvement strategies/plans	☒	☒

Analyst: Terminal Output

	Current Work	Future Work
95. Persuasive reports to stakeholders about past, present, and future performance gaps and their cause(s)	☐	☒

Intervention Specialist: Enabling Outputs

	Current Work	Future Work
96. Written or oral briefings to performers, performers' managers, process owners, or other stakeholders about the results of performance analysis or cause analysis	☐	☒
97. Useful information drawn from performance or cause analysis	☐	☒
98. Approaches for choosing appropriate human performance improvement strategies to close performance gaps	☐	☒

This worksheet is reproducible.

Enabling and Terminal Outputs Associated with HPI Roles	Current Work	Future Work
99. Written and oral briefings to performers, performers' managers, process owners, and other stakeholders about the likely impact of change or of a human performance improvement intervention on processes, individuals, or the organization	☐	☒
100. Problem-solving activities to lead performers, performers' managers, process owners, and other stakeholders to discover/forecast the impact of an intervention's implementation on processes, individuals, or the organization	☐	☒
101. Written and oral briefings to performers, performers' managers, process owners, and other stakeholders about the likely impact of multiple interventions on processes, individuals, or the organization	☐	☒
102. Problem-solving activities to lead performers, performers' managers, process owners, and other stakeholders to discover/forecast the likely impact of multiple interventions on processes, individuals, or the organization	☐	☒
103. Organizational analyses	☒	☒
104. Process analyses	☒	☒
105. Individual assessments	☒	☒
106. White papers on human performance improvement strategies	☒	☒
107. Oral and written briefings to performers, performers' managers, process owners, and other stakeholders about possible improvement strategies	☐	☒
108. Customer satisfaction information/survey results	☐	☒
109. Written or oral goals for human performance improvement	☐	☒
110. Performance objectives for interventions	☐	☒
111. Facilitated performance objectives	☒	☒
Intervention Specialist: Terminal Output 112. Persuasive reports to stakeholders about the appropriate intervention(s) to close past, present, or future performance gap(s)	☐	☒
Change Manager: Enabling Outputs 113. A convincing case made for the need for change	☐	☒
114. Organizational sponsorship identified and secured	☐	☒
115. Evidence of support obtained through commitment of resources	☐	☒
116. Designs/action plans for introducing and consolidating interventions	☐	☒
117. Designs/plans for reducing resistance to interventions	☐	☒

This worksheet is reproducible.

Worksheet 2: Profile of Enabling Outputs Associated with HPI Core Competencies (continued)

Enabling and Terminal Outputs Associated with HPI Roles	Current Work	Future Work
118. Recommendations to management about management's role in introducing and consolidating change	☐	☒
119. Recommendations to workers about their role in introducing and consolidating change	☐	☒
120. Communication plans established to keep participants in change and stakeholders of change informed about the progress of the human performance improvement intervention	☐	☒
121. Groups successfully observed	☐	☒
122. Plans for influencing groups based on knowledge of small group development theory	☐	☒
123. Group process observation forms	☐	☒
124. Descriptions to group members and individuals about the effects of their behavior on a group or on individuals	☐	☒
125. Plans for facilitating group discussions	☐	☒
126. Plans for facilitating individual or group decision making and problem solving	☐	☒
Change Manager: Terminal Outputs		
127. Performance improvement interventions effectively monitored with participants and stakeholders	☐	☒
128. Effective interpersonal interactions among participants and stakeholders of interventions	☐	☒
129. Tracking systems to compare actual and ideal performance and progress toward narrowing or closing performance gaps, or realizing performance opportunities as the intervention is implemented	☐	☒
130. Oral and/or written agreements among most or all stakeholders about the results desired from the intervention	☐	☒
131. Measurable financial or nonfinancial objectives to be achieved during and after implementation of the intervention(s)	☐	☒
Evaluator: Enabling Outputs		
132. Human performance improvement evaluation objectives	☒	☒
133. Human performance improvement evaluation designs and plans	☐	☒
134. Human performance improvement evaluation instruments	☐	☒
135. Pre- and post-measures of worker performance	☐	☒

This worksheet is reproducible.

Enabling and Terminal Outputs Associated with HPI Roles	Current Work	Future Work
136. Evaluation findings, conclusions, and recommendations	☐	☒
137. Reports to management and workers on the outcomes of human performance improvement strategies	☐	☒
138. Linkage of human performance improvement interventions to other change efforts of the organization	☐	☒
139. Linkage of each human performance improvement intervention with other interventions	☐	☒
140. Linkage of human performance improvement interventions to organizational plans, goals, and objectives	☐	☒
141. Linkage of human performance improvement interventions to organizational/business needs	☐	☒
142. Work standards/expectations established	☒	☒
143. Work standards/expectations communicated	☐	☒
144. Linkage of human performance improvement interventions to organizational culture	☐	☒
145. Written and oral reports to stakeholders/participants about the progress of an intervention	☐	☒
146. Feedback to the organization about performance	☐	☒
147. Feedback to the organization about progress of interventions	☐	☒
148. Feedback to work groups or teams about performance	☒	☒
149. Feedback to work groups or teams about progress of interventions	☐	☒
150. Feedback to management about performance	☐	☒
151. Feedback to management about interventions	☐	☒

Evaluator: Terminal Outputs

	Current Work	Future Work
152. Written and oral reports to participants and stakeholders about the progress of an intervention	☐	☒
153. Written or oral reports to the organization about performance	☐	☒
154. Written or oral reports to the organization about progress of interventions	☐	☒
155. Written or oral reports to work groups or teams about their performance	☐	☒
156. Written or oral reports to work groups or teams about the progress of interventions	☐	☒
157. Written or oral reports to management about performance	☐	☒
158. Written or oral reports to management about interventions	☐	☒

This worksheet is reproducible.

Worksheet 3: Self-Assessment Inventory

Rate yourself

1. Rate your expertise in each competency area by circling the appropriate number under "Current Level of Expertise." Use the following definitions to help you identify your level of expertise:

- ■ None (0): I have very little knowledge of, or experience in, applying this competency to HPI.

- ■ Basic (1-2): I possess general understanding of key principles, and I am capable of making simple decisions regarding the proper application of this competency to HPI.

- ■ Intermediate (3-4): I possess a comprehensive understanding of key principles, and I am capable of making complex decisions regarding the application of this competency to HPI

- ■ Advanced (5-6): I possess substantial knowledge and expertise and can work in complex situations that require the application of this competency to HPI.

Use the higher number if you feel strongly that you have reached this level of expertise. Use the lower number if you are less confident that you have reached this level.

2. Cover up your "Current Level of Expertise" answers. Go to the last column on the right and rate on a scale from 1 to 4 how important you think this competency is for your future success in the field of human performance improvement. This assessment should be completely independent of which competencies you think you already have or don't have. Here is what the numbers correspond to:

- ◆ 1: not important to future success

- ◆ 2: somewhat important to future success

- ◆ 3: important to future success

- ◆ 4: very important to future success

Worksheet 3: Self-Assessment Inventory

Core Competencies	Current Level of Expertise							Future Importance			
	None	Basic		Intermediate		Advanced		How important is this competency for future success?			
Industry Awareness: understanding the vision, strategy, goals, and culture of an industry; linking human performance improvement interventions to organizational goals	0	1 X	2	3	4	5	6	1	2	3	4
Leadership Skills: knowing how to lead or influence others positively to achieve desired work results	0	1	2 X	3	4	5	6	1	2	3	4
Interpersonal Relationship Skills: working effectively with others to achieve common goals and exercising effective interpersonal influence	0	1	2	3	4 X	5	6	1	2	3	4
Technological Awareness and Understanding: using existing or new technology and different types of software and hardware; understanding performance support systems and applying them as appropriate	0	1	2	3 X	4	5	6	1	2	3	4
Problem-Solving Skills: detecting performance gaps and helping other people discover ways to close the performance gaps in the present and future; closing performance gaps between actual and ideal performance	0	1	2	3 X	4 ▓	5	6	1	2	3	4
Systems Thinking and Understanding: identifying inputs, throughputs, and outputs of a subsystem, system, or suprasystem and applying that information to improve human performance; realizing the implications of interventions on many parts of an organization, process, or individual and taking steps to address any side effects of human performance improvement interventions	0	1	2	3 X	4	5	6	1	2	3	4
Performance Understanding: distinguishing between activities and results; recognizing implications, outcomes, and consequences	0	1	2 X	3	4	5	6	1	2	3	4

This worksheet is reproducible.

Worksheet 3: Self-Assessment Inventory (continued)

Core Competencies	Current Level of Expertise							Future Importance			
	None	Basic		Intermediate		Advanced		How important is this competency for future success?			
	0	1	2	3	4	5	6	1	2	3	4
Knowledge of Interventions: demonstrating an understanding of the many ways that human performance can be improved in organizational settings; showing how to apply specific human performance improvement interventions to close existing or anticipated performance gaps	0	1	2 X	3	4	5	6	1	2	3	4
Business Understanding: demonstrating awareness of the inner workings of business functions and how business decisions affect financial or nonfinancial work results (McLagan, 1989)	0	1	2	3	4 X	5	6	1	2	3	4
Organization Understanding: seeing organizations as dynamic, political, economic, and social systems that have multiple goals; using this larger perspective as a framework for understanding and influencing events and change (McLagan, 1989)	0	1	2	3	4 X	5	6	1	2	3	4
Negotiating/Contracting Skills: organizing, preparing, overseeing, and evaluating work performed by vendors, contingent workers, or outsourcing agents	0	1	2 X	3	4	5	6	1	2	3	4
Buy-in/Advocacy Skills: building ownership or support for change among affected individuals, groups, and other stakeholders	0	1	2	3 X	4	5	6	1	2	3	4
Coping Skills: knowing how to deal with ambiguity and how to handle the stress resulting from change and from multiple meanings or possibilities	0	1	2	3 X	4	5	6	1	2	3	4
Ability to See "Big Picture": looking beyond details to see overarching goals and results	0	1	2	3	4 X	5	6	1	2	3	4
Consulting Skills: understanding the results that stakeholders desire from a process and providing insight into how efficiently and effectively those results can be achieved	0	1	2 X	3	4	5	6	1	2	3	4

This worksheet is reproducible.

Role Competencies	Current Level of Expertise							Future Importance			
	None	Basic		Intermediate		Advanced		How important is this competency for future success?			
Analyst **Performance Analysis Skills (Front-End Analysis):** process of comparing actual and ideal performance in order to iden-tify performance gaps or opportunities	0	1	2 X	3	4	5	6	1	2	3	4
Needs Analysis Survey Design and Development Skills (Open-Ended and Structured): preparing written (mail), oral (phone), or electronic (e-mail) surveys using open-ended (essay) and closed (scaled) questions in order to identify human performance improvement needs	0	1 X	2	3	4	5	6	1	2	3	4
Competency Identification Skills: identifying the knowledge and skill requirements of teams, jobs, tasks, roles, and work (McLagan, 1989)	0	1	2 X	3	4	5	6	1	2	3	4
Questioning Skills: gathering pertinent information to stimulate insight in individuals and groups through use of interviews and other probing methods (McLagan, 1989)	0	1	2 X	3	4	5	6	1	2	3	4
Analytical Skills (Synthesis): breaking down the components of a larger whole and reassembling them to achieve improved human performance	0	1	2	3 X	4	5	6	1	2	3	4
Work Environment Analytical Skills: examining work environments for issues or characteristics affecting human performance	0	1	2 X	3	4	5	6	1	2	3	4

This worksheet is reproducible.

Worksheet 3: Self-Assessment Inventory (continued)

Role Competencies	Current Level of Expertise							Future Importance			
	None	Basic		Intermediate		Advanced		How important is this competency for future success?			
	0	1	2	3	4	5	6	1	2	3	4
Intervention Specialist **Performance Information Interpretation Skills:** finding useful meaning from the results of performance analysis and helping performers, performers' managers, process owners, and other stakeholders to do so	X										
Intervention Selection Skills: selecting human performance improvement interventions that address the root cause(s) of performance gaps rather than symptoms or side effects	X										
Performance Change Interpretation Skills: forecasting and analyzing the effects of interventions and their consequences	X										
Ability to Assess Relationships Among Interventions: examining the effects of multiple human performance improvement interventions on parts of an organization, as well as the effects on the organization's interactions with its customers, suppliers, distributors, and workers	X										
Ability to Identify Critical Business Issues and Changes: determining key business issues and applying that information during the implementation of a human performance improvement intervention	X										
Goal Implementation Skills: ensuring that goals are converted effectively into actions to close existing or pending performance gaps; getting results despite conflicting priorities, lack of resources, or ambiguity		X									

This worksheet is reproducible.

Role Competencies	Current Level of Expertise							Future Importance			
	None	Basic		Intermediate		Advanced		How important is this competency for future success?			
	0	1	2	3	4	5	6	1	2	3	4
Change Manager **Change Impetus Skills:** determining what the organization should do to address the cause(s) of a human performance gap at present and in the future	X										
Communication Channel, Informal Network, and Alliance Understanding: knowing how communication moves through an organization by various channels, networks, and alliances; building such channels, networks, and alliances to achieve improvements in productivity and performance			X								
Group Dynamics Process Understanding: understanding how groups function; influencing people so that group, work, and individual needs are addressed (McLagan, 1989)			X								
Process Consultation Skills: observing individuals and groups for their interactions and the effects of their interactions with others		X									
Facilitation Skills: helping performers, performers' managers, process owners, and stakeholders to discover new insights		X									

This worksheet is reproducible.

Worksheet 3: Self-Assessment Inventory (continued)

Role Competencies	Current Level of Expertise							Future Importance			
	None	Basic		Intermediate		Advanced		How important is this competency for future success?			
	0	**1**	**2**	**3**	**4**	**5**	**6**	**1**	**2**	**3**	**4**
Evaluator **Performance Gap Evaluation Skills:** measuring or helping others to measure the difference between actual performance and ideal performance	X										
Ability to Evaluate Results Against Organizational Goals: assessing how well the results of a human performance improvement intervention match intentions	X										
Standard Setting Skills: measuring desired results of organizations, processes, or individuals; helping others to establish and measure work expectations		X									
Ability to Assess Impact on Culture: examining the effects of human performance gaps and human performance improvement interventions on shared beliefs and assumptions about "right" and "wrong" ways of behaving and acting in one organizational setting	X										
Human Performance Improvement Intervention Reviewing Skills: finding ways to evaluate and continuously improve human performance improvement interventions before and during implementation	X										
Feedback Skills: collecting information about performance and feeding it back clearly, specifically, and on a timely basis to affected individuals or groups (McLagan, 1989)		X									

This worksheet is reproducible.

Worksheet 4: 360°–Assessment Inventory

On the following pages, you will find the assessment inventory that your peers, direct reports, and supervisor will use. At the top of the worksheet, respondents are given an opportunity to identify themselves and to state their relationship to you. Although this information is helpful, the respondents should be allowed to turn in the inventory anonymously. Only your supervisor must reveal his or her identity. We have also supplied you with a cover page that you can use when distributing the inventory. Here are some steps and important guidelines to remember:

Guidelines:

1. Ask people if they are interested in participating in this activity before you send them the inventory.

2. Tell them clearly what this inventory is being used for, how long it will take, and when it is due.

3. Advise respondents that they may turn in this inventory anonymously if they so choose. Let your supervisor know that his or her responses cannot be given anonymously.

4. Tell respondents that you want candid, future-focused feedback, but not a personality or performance appraisal. Make them comfortable with the idea of providing honest feedback. Tell them that after you've reviewed the completed assessment, you may come back to clarify, but not challenge, their responses (if they chose to put their name on the inventory).

Steps:

1. Make photocopies of the 360°–Assessment Inventory. You will need one copy for each respondent who you intend to have complete it.

2. Make photocopies of the cover sheet, which is on the next page. Be sure to address a cover sheet to each respondent, fill out the necessary information, and staple it to the front of the inventory.

3. Distribute the inventory to the respondents.

4. Send out a reminder notice a few days before the inventory is due.

5. Collect the inventories on the due date, and complete worksheet 5, "Summary of Results."

Cover Sheet for 360°–Assessment Inventory

From: _____ To: _____ Date: _____

Thank you for agreeing to participate in this competency assessment activity. I am trying to determine which competencies are strengths for me and which competencies I need to develop. Please give me candid, future-focused, and honest feedback of my competencies. Below is a full set of instructions. If you need any further clarification, feel free to call me at (_____) _____. The competencies that you are measuring me against were derived from the book *ASTD Models for Human Performance Improvement*. They describe the major competencies that are necessary to perform HPI work. If you have any difficulty understanding what these competencies are referring to, please call me for more information. Again, thank you for participating in this activity. The due date is _____.

> **Directions:** Please think about the person who has asked you to complete this assessment. You can help this person by giving him or her feedback based on your personal observations of his or her work. Although this questionnaire is not a performance appraisal, answering the following questions will provide helpful guidance for this person to develop into expanded roles within the organization. Here are the steps you need to follow.

1. Indicate in the first column if you have observed the person demonstrating the competency that is described. If you have not observed the person demonstrating this competency, skip to the next competency. If you have observed the person demonstrating this competency, go to step #2.

2. On a scale from 0 to 6, give the person an idea of how proficient he or she is in this competency. Use the following definitions to help you identify the person's level of expertise:

◆ None (0): Possesses very little knowledge of, or experience in, applying this competency to HPI work.
◆ Basic (1-2): Possesses general understanding of key principles and is capable of making simple decisions regarding the proper application of this competency to HPI work.
◆ Intermediate (3-4): Possesses a comprehensive understanding of key principles and is capable of making complex decisions regarding the application of this competency to HPI work.
◆ Advanced (5-6): Possesses substantial knowledge and expertise and can work in complex situations that require the application of this competency to HPI work.

Use the higher number if you feel strongly that the person has reached this level of expertise. Use the lower number if you are less confident that he or she has reached this level. You will need the following definitions to help you in this assessment:

Competencies: "Internal capabilities that people bring to their jobs. They may be expressed in a broad, even infinite, array of on-the-job behaviors." (McLagan, 1989, p. 77). The skills and knowledge people need to successfully do their jobs.

Human performance improvement: The systematic process of discovering and analyzing important human performance gaps, planning for future improvements in human performance, designing and developing cost-effective and ethically justifiable interventions to close performance gaps, implementing the interventions, and evaluating the financial and nonfinancial results.

3. Finally, cover up the "Current Level of Expertise" answers. Go to the last column on the right and rate on a scale from 1 to 4 how important you think this competency is for the person's future success in the field of human performance improvement. **Remember, this assessment should be completely independent of which competencies you think the person being rated already has or does not have.** Here is what the numbers correspond to:

◆ 1: not important to future success
◆ 2: somewhat important to future success
◆ 3: important to future success
◆ 4: very important to future success

Example:

Worksheet 4: 360°–Assessment Inventory

General Competencies		Have they demonstrated this competency?	Current Level of Expertise							Future Importance			
			None	Basic		Intermediate		Advanced		How important is this competency for future success?			
Leadership Skills: knowing how to lead or influence others positively to achieve desired work results		☑ Yes ☐ No	0	1	2	3	(4)	5	6	1	2	(3)	4

Name of Person Being Reviewed: _____ Date: _____

Reviewer's Name (optional): _____

Relationship: The person being reviewed is my:　　❏ Direct Report　　　❏ Peer　　　❏ Supervisor

Worksheet 4: 360°–Assessment Inventory

Core Competencies	Have they demonstrated this competency?	Current Level of Expertise							Future Importance
		None	Basic		Intermediate		Advanced		How important is this competency for future success?
Industry Awareness: understanding the vision, strategy, goals, and culture of an industry; linking human performance improvement interventions to organizational goals	❏ Yes ❏ No	0	1	2	3	4	5	6	1　2　3　4
Leadership Skills: knowing how to lead or influence others positively to achieve desired work results	❏ Yes ❏ No	0	1	2	3	4	5	6	1　2　3　4
Interpersonal Relationship Skills: working effectively with others to achieve common goals and exercising effective interpersonal influence	❏ Yes ❏ No	0	1	2	3	4	5	6	1　2　3　4
Technological Awareness and Understanding: using existing or new technology and different types of software and hardware; understanding performance support systems and applying them as appropriate	❏ Yes ❏ No	0	1	2	3	4	5	6	1　2　3　4
Problem-Solving Skills: detecting performance gaps and helping other people discover ways to close the performance gaps in the present and future; closing performance gaps between actual and ideal performance	❏ Yes ❏ No	0	1	2	3	4	5	6	1　2　3　4
Systems Thinking and Understanding: identifying inputs, throughputs, and outputs of a subsystem, system, or supra-system and applying that information to improve human performance; realizing the implications of interventions on many parts of an organization, process, or individual and taking steps to address any side effects of human performance improvement interventions	❏ Yes ❏ No	0	1	2	3	4	5	6	1　2　3　4
Performance Understanding: distinguishing between activities and results; recognizing implications, outcomes, and consequences	❏ Yes ❏ No	0	1	2	3	4	5	6	1　2　3　4

This worksheet is reproducible.

Core Competencies	Have they demonstrated this competency?	Current Level of Expertise							Future Importance
		None	Basic		Intermediate		Advanced		How important is this competency for future success?
		0	1	2	3	4	5	6	1 2 3 4
Knowledge of Interventions: demonstrating an understanding of the many ways that human performance can be improved in organizational settings; showing how to apply specific human performance improvement interventions to close existing or anticipated performance gaps	❏ Yes ❏ No	0	1	2	3	4	5	6	1 2 3 4
Business Understanding: demonstrating awareness of the inner workings of business functions and how business decisions affect financial or nonfinancial work results (McLagan, 1989)	❏ Yes ❏ No	0	1	2	3	4	5	6	1 2 3 4
Organization Understanding: seeing organizations as dynamic, political, economic, and social systems that have multiple goals; using this larger perspective as a framework for understanding and influencing events and change (McLagan, 1989)	❏ Yes ❏ No	0	1	2	3	4	5	6	1 2 3 4
Negotiating/Contracting Skills: organizing, preparing, overseeing, and evaluating work performed by vendors, contingent workers, or outsourcing agents	❏ Yes ❏ No	0	1	2	3	4	5	6	1 2 3 4
Buy-in/Advocacy Skills: building ownership or support for change among affected individuals, groups, and other stakeholders	❏ Yes ❏ No	0	1	2	3	4	5	6	1 2 3 4
Coping Skills: knowing how to deal with ambiguity and how to handle the stress resulting from change and from multiple meanings or possibilities	❏ Yes ❏ No	0	1	2	3	4	5	6	1 2 3 4
Ability to See "Big Picture": looking beyond details to see overarching goals and results	❏ Yes ❏ No	0	1	2	3	4	5	6	1 2 3 4
Consulting Skills: understanding the results that stakeholders desire from a process and providing insight into how efficiently and effectively those results can be achieved	❏ Yes ❏ No	0	1	2	3	4	5	6	1 2 3 4

This worksheet is reproducible.

Role Competencies	Have they demonstrated this competency?	Current Level of Expertise							Future Importance
		None	Basic		Intermediate		Advanced		How important is this competency for future success?

Analyst

Role Competencies	Have they demonstrated this competency?	None	Basic		Intermediate		Advanced		Future Importance
Analyst **Performance Analysis Skills (Front-End Analysis):** process of comparing actual and ideal performance in order to iden-tify performance gaps or opportunities	❑ Yes ❑ No	0	1	2	3	4	5	6	1 2 3 4
Needs Analysis Survey Design and Development Skills (Open-Ended and Structured): preparing written (mail), oral (phone), or electronic (e-mail) surveys using open-ended (essay) and closed (scaled) questions in order to identify human performance improvement needs	❑ Yes ❑ No	0	1	2	3	4	5	6	1 2 3 4
Competency Identification Skills: identifying the knowledge and skill requirements of teams, jobs, tasks, roles, and work (McLagan, 1989)	❑ Yes ❑ No	0	1	2	3	4	5	6	1 2 3 4
Questioning Skills: gathering pertinent information to stimulate insight in individuals and groups through use of interviews and other probing methods (McLagan, 1989)	❑ Yes ❑ No	0	1	2	3	4	5	6	1 2 3 4
Analytical Skills (Synthesis): breaking down the components of a larger whole and reassembling them to achieve improved human performance	❑ Yes ❑ No	0	1	2	3	4	5	6	1 2 3 4
Work Environment Analytical Skills: examining work environments for issues or characteristics affecting human performance	❑ Yes ❑ No	0	1	2	3	4	5	6	1 2 3 4

This worksheet is reproducible.

Role Competencies	Have they demonstrated this competency?	Current Level of Expertise							Future Importance
		None	Basic		Intermediate		Advanced		How important is this competency for future success?
Intervention Specialist **Performance Information Interpretation Skills:** finding useful meaning from the results of performance analysis and helping performers, performers' managers, process owners, and other stakeholders to do so	❏ Yes ❏ No	0	1	2	3	4	5	6	1 2 3 4
Intervention Selection Skills: selecting human performance improvement interventions that address the root cause(s) of performance gaps rather than symptoms or side effects	❏ Yes ❏ No	0	1	2	3	4	5	6	1 2 3 4
Performance Change Interpretation Skills: forecasting and analyzing the effects of interventions and their consequences	❏ Yes ❏ No	0	1	2	3	4	5	6	1 2 3 4
Ability to Assess Relationships Among Interventions: examining the effects of multiple human performance improvement interventions on parts of an organization, as well as the effects on the organization's interactions with its customers, suppliers, distributors, and workers	❏ Yes ❏ No	0	1	2	3	4	5	6	1 2 3 4
Ability to Identify Critical Business Issues and Changes: determining key business issues and applying that information during the implementation of a human performance improvement intervention	❏ Yes ❏ No	0	1	2	3	4	5	6	1 2 3 4
Goal Implementation Skills: ensuring that goals are converted effectively into actions to close existing or pending performance gaps; getting results despite conflicting priorities, lack of resources, or ambiguity	❏ Yes ❏ No	0	1	2	3	4	5	6	1 2 3 4

This worksheet is reproducible.

Role Competencies	Have they demonstrated this competency?	Current Level of Expertise							Future Importance
		None	Basic		Intermediate		Advanced		How important is this competency for future success?
Change Manager **Change Impetus Skills:** determining what the organization should do to address the cause(s) of a human performance gap at present and in the future	❑ **Yes** ❑ **No**	0	1	2	3	4	5	6	1 2 3 4
Communication Channel, Informal Network, and Alliance Understanding: knowing how communication moves through an organization by various channels, networks, and alliances; building such channels, networks, and alliances to achieve improvements in productivity and performance	❑ **Yes** ❑ **No**	0	1	2	3	4	5	6	1 2 3 4
Group Dynamics Process Understanding: understanding how groups function; influencing people so that group, work, and individual needs are addressed (McLagan, 1989)	❑ **Yes** ❑ **No**	0	1	2	3	4	5	6	1 2 3 4
Process Consultation Skills: observing individuals and groups for their interactions and the effects of their interactions with others	❑ **Yes** ❑ **No**	0	1	2	3	4	5	6	1 2 3 4
Facilitation Skills: helping performers, performers' managers, process owners, and stakeholders to discover new insights	❑ **Yes** ❑ **No**	0	1	2	3	4	5	6	1 2 3 4

This worksheet is reproducible.

Role Competencies	Have they demonstrated this competency?	Current Level of Expertise							Future Importance
		None	Basic		Intermediate		Advanced		How important is this competency for future success?

Evaluator

Performance Gap Evaluation Skills: measuring or helping others to measure the difference between actual performance and ideal performance
❑ Yes ❑ No — 0 1 2 3 4 5 6 — 1 2 3 4

Ability to Evaluate Results Against Organizational Goals: assessing how well the results of a human performance improvement intervention match intentions
❑ Yes ❑ No — 0 1 2 3 4 5 6 — 1 2 3 4

Standard Setting Skills: measuring desired results of organizations, processes, or individuals; helping others to establish and measure work expectations
❑ Yes ❑ No — 0 1 2 3 4 5 6 — 1 2 3 4

Ability to Assess Impact on Culture: examining the effects of human performance gaps and human performance improvement interventions on shared beliefs and assumptions about "right" and "wrong" ways of behaving and acting in one organizational setting
❑ Yes ❑ No — 0 1 2 3 4 5 6 — 1 2 3 4

Human Performance Improvement Intervention Reviewing Skills: finding ways to evaluate and continuously improve human performance improvement interventions before and during implementation
❑ Yes ❑ No — 0 1 2 3 4 5 6 — 1 2 3 4

Feedback Skills: collecting information about performance and feeding it back clearly, specifically, and on a timely basis to affected individuals or groups (McLagan, 1989)
❑ Yes ❑ No — 0 1 2 3 4 5 6 — 1 2 3 4

This worksheet is reproducible.

Worksheet 5: Summary of Results

Use the worksheet below to summarize and analyze the results of your data collection. Here are the steps you want to follow:

1. Each competency below has two rows for entering data. In the top row, enter the assessment scores that you received for your current level of expertise. (1–6) In the bottom row, enter the assessment scores for the future importance of the competency. (1–4)

2. For each "current level" row, write in all of the scores that you received from your direct reports in the cell provided. Do the same for your self-assessment scores, all of your peers' scores, and your supervisor's score. If a respondent checked "no" in the second column for a competency in the Assessment

Inventory, do not include a score for that item, and divide the total score by one less response.

3. Add all the scores together, and write the total in the appropriate cell.

4. Divide the sum total by the number of responses that you received. Write the average in the appropriate cell, (last column on the right).

5. Repeat the above steps for the "future importance" scores for each competency.

Example:

Worksheet 5: Summary of Results

Core Competencies		Direct Reports	Self	Peers	Supervisor	Totals	Averages
Leadership Skills: knowing how to lead or influence others positively to achieve desired work results	Current	5, 6, 3	2	4, 5, 5	6	36	4.5
	Future	4, 3, 4	3	4, 4, 5	2	29	3.63

Core Competencies		Direct Reports	Self	Peers	Supervisor	Totals	Averages
Industry Awareness: understanding the vision, strategy, goals, and culture of an industry; linking human performance improvement interventions to organizational goals	Current						
	Future						
Leadership Skills: knowing how to lead or influence others positively to achieve desired work results	Current						
	Future						
Interpersonal Relationship Skills: working effectively with others to achieve common goals and exercising effective interpersonal influence	Current						
	Future						
Technological Awareness and Understanding: using existing or new technology and different types of software and hardware; understanding performance support systems and applying them as appropriate	Current						
	Future						
Problem-Solving Skills: detecting performance gaps and helping other people discover ways to close the performance gaps in the present and future; closing performance gaps between actual and ideal performance	Current						
	Future						
Systems Thinking and Understanding: identifying inputs, throughputs, and outputs of a subsystem, system, or suprasystem and applying that information to improve human performance; realizing the implications of interventions on many parts of an organization, process, or individual and taking steps to address any side effects of human performance improvement interventions	Current						
	Future						
Performance Understanding: distinguishing between activities and results; recognizing implications, outcomes, and consequences	Current						
	Future						

This worksheet is reproducible.

Core Competencies		Direct Reports	Self	Peers	Supervisor	Totals	Averages
Knowledge of Interventions: demonstrating an understanding of the many ways that human performance can be improved in organizational settings; showing how to apply specific human performance improvement interventions to close existing or anticipated performance gaps	Current						
	Future						
Business Understanding: demonstrating awareness of the inner workings of business functions and how business decisions affect financial or nonfinancial work results (McLagan, 1989)	Current						
	Future						
Organization Understanding: seeing organizations as dynamic, political, economic, and social systems that have multiple goals; using this larger perspective as a framework for understanding and influencing events and change (McLagan, 1989)	Current						
	Future						
Negotiating/Contracting Skills: organizing, preparing, overseeing, and evaluating work performed by vendors, contingent workers, or outsourcing agents	Current						
	Future						
Buy-in/Advocacy Skills: building ownership or support for change among affected individuals, groups, and other stakeholders	Current						
	Future						
Coping Skills: knowing how to deal with ambiguity and how to handle the stress resulting from change and from multiple meanings or possibilities	Current						
	Future						
Ability to See "Big Picture": looking beyond details to see overarching goals and results	Current						
	Future						
Consulting Skills: understanding the results that stakeholders desire from a process and providing insight into how efficiently and effectively those results can be achieved	Current						
	Future						

This worksheet is reproducible.

Role Competencies		Direct Reports	Self	Peers	Supervisor	Totals	Averages
Analyst **Performance Analysis Skills (Front-End Analysis):** process of comparing actual and ideal performance in order to identify performance gaps or opportunities	Current						
	Future						
Needs Analysis Survey Design and Development Skills (Open-Ended and Structured): preparing written (mail), oral (phone), or electronic (e-mail) surveys using open-ended (essay) and closed (scaled) questions in order to identify human performance improvement needs	Current						
	Future						
Competency Identification Skills: identifying the knowledge and skill requirements of teams, jobs, tasks, roles, and work (McLagan, 1989)	Current						
	Future						
Questioning Skills: gathering pertinent information to stimulate insight in individuals and groups through use of interviews and other probing methods (McLagan, 1989)	Current						
	Future						
Analytical Skills (Synthesis): breaking down the components of a larger whole and reassembling them to achieve improved human performance	Current						
	Future						
Work Environment Analytical Skills: examining work environments for issues or characteristics affecting human performance	Current						
	Future						

This worksheet is reproducible.

Role Competencies		Direct Reports	Self	Peers	Supervisor	Totals	Averages
Intervention Specialist **Performance Information Interpretation Skills:** finding useful meaning from the results of performance analysis and helping performers, performers' managers, process owners, and other stakeholders to do so	Current						
	Future						
Intervention Selection Skills: selecting human performance improvement interventions that address the root cause(s) of performance gaps rather than symptoms or side effects	Current						
	Future						
Performance Change Interpretation Skills: forecasting and analyzing the effects of interventions and their consequences	Current						
	Future						
Ability to Assess Relationships Among Interventions: examining the effects of multiple human performance improvement interventions on parts of an organization, as well as the effects on the organization's interactions with its customers, suppliers, distributors, and workers	Current						
	Future						
Ability to Identify Critical Business Issues and Changes: determining key business issues and applying that information during the implementation of a human performance improvement intervention	Current						
	Future						
Goal Implementation Skills: ensuring that goals are converted effectively into actions to close existing or pending performance gaps; getting results despite conflicting priorities, lack of resources, or ambiguity	Current						
	Future						

This worksheet is reproducible.

Role Competencies		Direct Reports	Self	Peers	Supervisor	Totals	Averages
Change Manager **Change Impetus Skills:** determining what the organization should do to address the cause(s) of a human performance gap at present and in the future	Current						
	Future						
Communication Channel, Informal Network, and Alliance Understanding: knowing how communication moves through an organization by various channels, networks, and alliances; building such channels, networks, and alliances to achieve improvements in productivity and performance	Current						
	Future						
Group Dynamics Process Understanding: understanding how groups function; influencing people so that group, work, and individual needs are addressed (McLagan, 1989)	Current						
	Future						
Process Consultation Skills: observing individuals and groups for their interactions and the effects of their interactions with others	Current						
	Future						
Facilitation Skills: helping performers, performers' managers, process owners, and stakeholders to discover new insights	Current						
	Future						

This worksheet is reproducible.

Role Competencies		Direct Reports	Self	Peers	Supervisor	Totals	Averages
Evaluator **Performance Gap Evaluation Skills:** measuring or helping others to measure the difference between actual performance and ideal performance	Current						
	Future						
Ability to Evaluate Results Against Organizational Goals: assessing how well the results of a human performance improvement intervention match intentions	Current						
	Future						
Standard Setting Skills: measuring desired results of organizations, processes, or individuals; helping others to establish and measure work expectations	Current						
	Future						
Ability to Assess Impact on Culture: examining the effects of human performance gaps and human performance improvement interventions on shared beliefs and assumptions about "right" and "wrong" ways of behaving and acting in one organizational setting	Current						
	Future						
Human Performance Improvement Intervention Reviewing Skills: finding ways to evaluate and continuously improve human performance improvement interventions before and during implementation	Current						
	Future						
Feedback Skills: collecting information about performance and feeding it back clearly, specifically, and on a timely basis to affected individuals or groups (McLagan, 1989)	Current						
	Future						

This worksheet is reproducible.

1. Based on the current and future average scores from the first part of this worksheet, plot each competency's position on the graph supplied below. Draw a dot and the number of the competency in the appropriate place on the chart. For example, if "leadership skills" (competency #2) had an average current score of "4.5" and an average future score of "3.63" it would appear as shown below.

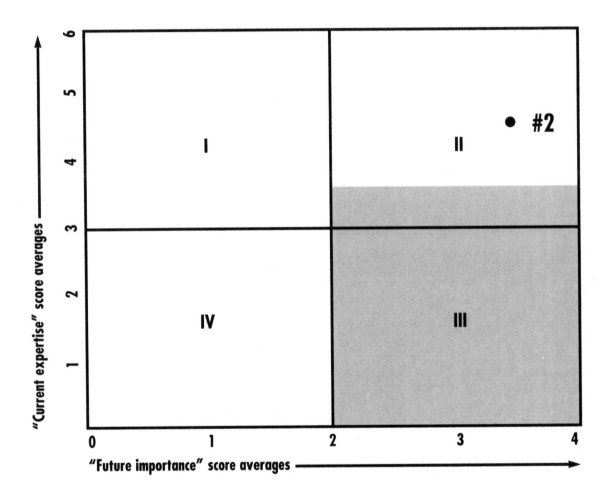

Once you have plotted all 38 competencies, take a long look at the chart. The competencies that fall within the shaded area are the ones that the average respondent thought to be very important to future success in the field. These are also the competencies that require the greatest amount of development. In particular, the closer the competency is to the lower, right corner of the graph, the more immediate the developmental need.

2. Based on the information from above, list some ideas that you have for developing the competencies that fall within the shaded area:

_____

_____

_____

_____

3. Go back and compare your self-assessment score for each competency to the average score. Write down all of the competencies below where your self-assessment score is more than two points higher or lower than the average. Next to each competency, write down some reasons why your self-assessment was so much different than the average assessment.

Competency Name: _____ Reason for difference: _____

Competency Name: _____ Reason for difference: _____

Competency Name: _____ Reason for difference: _____

Competency Name: _____ Reason for difference: _____

Competency Name: _____ Reason for difference: _____

Competency Name: _____ Reason for difference: _____

4. Consider all of the information above, and then create a list of objectives that would move you toward greater expertise in important competency areas. Use more paper if necessary.

Objective #1: _____

Objective #2: _____

Objective #3: _____

Objective #4: _____

This worksheet is reproducible.

Worksheet 6: Development Planning Tool

There are many ways to build new competencies, and many resources are available to help in that process. The following is a brief review of some possible ways:

- Talk to other people.
- Work with other people on short-term or long-term projects.
- Observe and learn from role models.
- Participate in formal or informal learning groups.
- Attend college courses.
- Participate in online courses.
- Search the Internet on topics that are related to human performance improvement.
- Attend nondegree continuing education seminars.
- Participate in professional associations.
- Use networks (online or interpersonal).
- Read periodicals, journals, or newsletters.
- Read books.
- Watch videotapes.
- Listen to audiotapes.
- Use software or multimedia-based learning methods.
- Attend conferences.

Use the following worksheet to generate ideas on how to develop the competencies that are necessary for success in the field of human performance improvement. Here are the steps you should follow:

1. List a competency that you need to develop and consider how to use the suggestions listed in the left column.

2. Make notes in the right column about ways to implement the suggestions in order to build proficiency.

3. Remember that there are not any "right" or "wrong" answers.

4. Add more paper if needed.

Example:

Competency Name: _____ *Leadership Skills* _____

Example:

Ways to Build the Competency	Ideas on How to Implement Suggestions
• *Talk to other people.*	• *Get Joe's suggestions on how to build this competency.*
	• *Ask Mary about that course she took on leadership skills.*
	• *Call ASTD and see if they will give me an information interview over the phone.*

This worksheet is reproducible.

Competency Name: _____

Ways to Build the Competency	Ideas on How to Implement Suggestions
• Talk to other people.	• • •
• Work with other people on short-term or long-term projects.	• • •
• Observe and learn from role models.	• • •
• Participate in formal or informal learning groups.	• • •
• Attend college courses.	• • •
• Participate in online courses.	• • •
• Search the Internet on topics that are related to human performance improvement.	• • •
• Attend nondegree continuing education seminars.	• • •
• Participate in professional associations.	• • •
• Use networks (online or interpersonal).	• • •
• Read periodicals, journals, or newsletters.	• • •
• Read books.	• • •
• Watch videotapes.	• • •
• Listen to audiotapes	• • •
• Use software or multimedia-based learning methods.	• • •
• Attend conferences	• • •

This worksheet is reproducible.

Worksheet 7: Learning Contract

The idea behind a learning contract is to formalize your objectives into a plan of action. This can be a very valuable tool for gaining the support of your supervisor, your co-workers, and your organization. It also will help you to track your progress toward your goals. To complete this learning contract, follow these steps:

1. Using your objectives from question 4 at the end of the second part of worksheet 5 (page 37), fill out your first objective for bridging the gaps between your current competencies and the competencies that you will need for future success. You will need a separate copy of the following worksheet for each objective that you state.

2. Fill in each activity that you believe will be needed in order to accomplish this objective.

3. Go back and estimate the amount of time each activity will take, the projected date for when it will be completed, what the deliverable will be (in other words, the output), what evaluation criteria will be used to judge it, who will evaluate it, what resources will be needed, and what obstacles you may encounter.

4. When you have completed one worksheet for each objective, make an appointment to discuss each of your objectives with your supervisor.

5. Negotiate the terms of the learning contract with your supervisor, update the learning contract, and get all parties involved to sign and date the document.

Example:

Objective #1 *To attain a higher level of competence in leadership skills.*

Activities	Date/Number of Hours	Deliverable	Evaluation Criteria	Evaluator	Resources	Obstacles
Read Stephen Covey's book "7 Habits of Highly Effective People."	Finish by 12/15. 15 hours	2-3 page paper	• Clearly written. • Accurately describes the book. • Makes logical connection to my job.	My supervisor	7 Habits of Highly Effective People	• Not being able to make logical connections to my job. • Not finding enough time to read the book

Employee's Signature: _____ Date: _____

Supervisor's Signature: _____ Date: _____

This worksheet is reproducible.

Worksheet 7: Learning Contract

Objective # _____

Activities	Date/Number of Hours	Deliverable	Evaluation Criteria	Evaluator	Resources	Obstacles

Employee's Signature: _____ Date: _____

Supervisor's Signature: _____ Date: _____

This worksheet is reproducible.

Preparation for the Future

Use this worksheet to prepare for managing future trends as they unfold.

Worksheet 8: Preparation for the Future

Directions: For each trend listed in column 1, indicate in column 2 what job categories or groups inside the organization are most likely to be affected by the trend. Then, in column 3, list the performance gaps that will likely be created by the trend. In column 4, indicate when the gaps' effects will be most keenly felt. Indicate in column 5 where (geographically) in the organization its gaps' effects will be greatest, and note why the gaps are important to the organization in column 6. In column 7, indicate how the organization should attempt to close the gaps through human performance improvement strategies.

Column 1	Column 2	Column 3	Column 4	Column 5	Column 6	Column 7
Trend	What job categories or groups inside the organization are most likely to be affected by the trend?	What performance gaps will likely be created by the trend?	When will the gaps' effects be most keenly felt	Where (geographically) in the organization will the gaps' effects be greatest?	Why are the gaps' effects important to the organization?	How should the organization attempt to close the gaps through human performance improvement strategies?
1. Performance						
2. Learning						
3. Business Trends						
4. Technology						
5. Structure of Training Organizations						

This worksheet is reproducible.

Ethical Dilemmas

Use this worksheet when you confront an ethical dilemma or ethical issue in the course of doing human performance improvement work.

Worksheet 9: Resolving Ethical Dilemmas

Directions: First describe the dilemma. Then try to describe the reasons for it. Answer the remaining questions appearing in the left column. When you finish, discuss the completed worksheet with supervisors, colleagues, co-workers, and other appropriate people. Add paper as necessary.

1. Describe the ethical dilemma or issue.

Questions About the Ethical Dilemma or Issue	Your Answers
2. What facts are relevant to the ethical dilemma or issue? (Describe them.)	
3. What are the ethical issues? (What issues are related to the situation at all organizational levels?)	
4. Who are the primary stakeholders? (Who is involved in the dilemma and/or is affected by the outcomes?)	
5. What are the appropriate actions to take to resolve the ethical dilemma or issue? (Make a list of alternative courses of action and their likely outcomes and impacts.)	
6. What are the likely ethical implications of each alternative identified in #5?	
7. What practical constraints limit the implementation of any alternative you identified in response to #5?	
8. What action should be taken and why?	

Adapted from Arthur Andersen Business Ethics Program by Patricia Werhane. Werhane, P. (1992). Corporate Moral and Social Responsibility. *Paper presented at Ethics Practice and Teaching Workshop. Colorado Springs, CO.*

This worksheet is reproducible.

Resources to build human performance improvement competencies. Consider the following resources, categorized by human performance improvement role, to help you expand your human performance improvement competencies.

Table 9.1: Information Sources Categorized by HPI Role

Roles	Possible Resources
Analyst	• Dean, P. (Ed.). (1994). *Performance engineering at work.* Batavia, IL: International Board of Standards for Training, Performance, and Instruction. • Dubois, D. (1993). *Competency-based performance improvement.* Amherst, MA: Human Resource Development Press. • Gilbert, T. (1978). *Human competence: Engineering worthy performance.* New York: McGraw-Hill. • Harless, J. (1975). *An ounce of analysis is worth a pound of objectives.* Newnan, GA: Guild V. Publications. • Mager, R., & Pipe, P. (1984). *Analyzing performance problems.* Belmont, CA: Lake. • Mills, G., Pace, W., & Peterson, B. (1988). *Analysis in human resource training and development.* Reading, MA: Addison-Wesley. • Rhinesmith, S. (1994). Reinventing the profession. 45-minute videotape. Alexandria, VA: The American Society for Training and Development. • Robinson, D., & Robinson, J. (1995). *Performance consulting: Moving beyond training.* San Francisco: Berrett-Koehler. • Rossett, A. (1990). *Training needs assessment.* Englewood Cliffs, NJ: Educational Technology Publications. • Stolovich, H., & Keeps, E. (Eds.). *Handbook of human performance technology: A comprehensive guide for analyzing and solving performance problems in organizations.* San Francisco: Jossey-Bass. • Swanson, R. (1994). *Analysis for improving performance: Tools for diagnosing organizations and documenting workplace expertise.* San Francisco: Berrett-Koehler. • Whiteley, R. (1991). *The customer-driven company: Moving from talk to action.* Reading, MA: Addison-Wesley.
Intervention Specialist	• Argyris, C. (1970). *Intervention theory and method.* Reading, MA: Addison-Wesley. • Barger, N., & Kirby, L. (1995). *The challenge of change in organizations: Helping employees thrive in the new frontier.* NC: Davies-Black Publishing. • Camp, R. (1989). *Benchmarking: The search for industry best practices that lead to superior performance.* Milwaukee, WI: ASQC Quality Press. • Clark, D., & Crossland, L. (1985). *Action systems: An introduction to the analysis of complex behavior.* London: Methuen. • Golembiewski, R. (Ed.). (1993). *Handbook of organizational consultation.* New York: Marcel Dekker, Inc. • Gouillart, F., & Kelly, J. (1995). *Transforming the organization: Reframing corporate direction, restructuring the company, revitalizing the enterprise, renewing people.* New York: McGraw-Hill. • Gradous, D. (Ed.). (1989). *Systems theory applied to human resource development.* Alexandria, VA: The American Society for Training and Development. • Harrington, H. (1992). *Business process improvement: The breakthrough strategy for total quality, productivity, and competitiveness.* New York: McGraw-Hill. • Holtz, H. (1993). *How to succeed as an independent consultant* (3rd ed.). New York: Wiley. • Kaufman, R. (1992). *Strategic planning: An organizational guide* (rev. ed.). Newbury Park, CA: Sage Publications. • Powers, B. (1992). Strategic alignment. In Stolovich, H., & Keeps, E. (Eds.). *Handbook of human performance technology: A comprehensive guide for analyzing and solving performance problems in organizations* (pp. 247-258). San Francisco: Jossey-Bass. • Rothwell, W., & Kazanas, H. (1994). *Human resource development: A strategic approach* (rev. ed.). Amherst, MA: Human Resource Development Press. • Rothwell, W., Sullivan, R., & McLean, G. (Eds.). (1995). *Practicing organization development: A guide for consultants.* San Diego: Pfeiffer & Co. • Rummler, G., & Brache, A. (1990). *Improving performance: How to manage the white space on the organization chart.* San Francisco: Jossey-Bass. • Smalley, K., Inman, S., & DeJong, M. (1995). "Strategic planning: From training to performance technology within three years." *Performance Improvement Quarterly,* 8(2), 114-124. • Ziegenfuss, J., Jr. (1988). *Organizational troubleshooters: Resolving problems with customers and employees.* San Francisco: Jossey-Bass.

Roles	Possible Resources

Change Manager

- American Society for Training and Development. (1992). *The best of…organizational change.* Alexandria, VA.
- Berger, L. A., Sikora, M. J., and Berger, D. R. (1994). *The change management handbook: A road map to corporate transformation.* Burr Ridge, IL: Irwin.
- Blohowiak, D. (1995). *How's all the work going to get done? How to manage the challenges of churning out more work with less staff.* NC: Career Press.
- Boyd, C. (1992). *Individual commitment and organizational change: A guide for human resource and organizational development specialists.* New York: Quorum.
- Connor, D. R. (1993). *Managing at the speed of change: How resilient managers succeed and prosper where others fail.* New York: Villard.
- Green, A. (1996). *A company discovers its soul: A year in the life of a transforming organization.* San Francisco, CA: Berrett-Koehler.
- Kissler, G. D. (1991). *The change riders: Managing the power of change.* Reading, MA: Addison-Wesley.
- Larkin, T. J., and Larkin, S. (1994). *Communicating change: How to win employee support for new business directions.* New York: McGraw-Hill.
- Lulic, M. A. (1994). *Who we could be at work.* Minneapolis, MN: Blue Edge.
- Overholt, M. (1996). *Building flexible organizations: A people-centered approach.* NC: Kendall/Hunt Publishing Co.
- Porter, M. (1980). *Competitive strategy: Techniques for analyzing industries and competitors.* New York: The Free Press.
- Rivto, R. A., Litwin, A. H., and Butler, L. (1995). *Managing in the age of change.* Burr Ridge, IL: Irwin.
- Schiller, S. (1994). *Dispelling the megatrends myth: A leader's guide to managing change.* Alexandria, VA: The Schiller Center.
- Smith, D. K. (1996). *Taking charge of change: 10 principles for managing people and performance.* Reading, MA: Addison-Wesley.
- Woodward, H. (1994). *Navigating through change.* Homewood, IL: Irwin.

Evaluator

- American Society for Training and Development. (1991). *The best of…the evaluation of training.* Alexandria, VA.
- Basarab, D. J., and Root, D. K. (1992). *The training evaluation process: A practical approach to evaluation corporate training programs.* Norwell, MA: Kluwer Academic.
- Holcomb, J. (1994). *Make training worth every penny: On-target evaluation.* San Diego, CA: Pfeiffer.
- Kirkpatrick, D. L. (1994). *Evaluating training programs: The four levels.* San Francisco, CA: Berrett-Koehler.
- Medsker, K. L., and Roberts, D. G. (eds.) (1992). *ASTD trainer's toolkit: Evaluating the results of training.* Alexandria, VA: American Society for Training and Development.
- Michalko, M. (1991). *Thinkertoys: A handbook of business creativity for the '90s.* Berkeley, CA: Ten Speed Press.
- Phillips, J. (1991). *Handbook of training evaluation and measurement methods* (2nd ed.). Houston, TX: Gulf Publishing.
- Rothwell, W. (1996). *Beyond training and development: State-of-the-art strategies for enhancing human performance.* New York: AMACOM.
- Swanson, R., & Gradous, D. (1988). *Forecasting financial benefits of human resource development.* San Francisco: Jossey-Bass.
- Thiagarajan, S. Formative evaluation in performance technology. *Performance Improvement Quarterly,* 4(2), 22-34.
- Zemke, R., and Kramlinger, T. (1982). Looking at performance. *Figuring things out.* Reading, MA: Addison-Wesley.

The Authors

William J. Rothwell is professor of human resource development in the Department of Adult Education, Instructional Systems, and Workforce Education and Development at the University Park campus of Pennsylvania State University. Rothwell is also director of the Institute for Research in Training and Development at Penn State.

Ethan S. Sanders is currently a project manager for the American Society for Training & Development. Before joining ASTD he was a senior instructional designer of management development courses in the banking industry. He also coauthored the ASTD course "Human Performance Improvement in the Workplace." He holds a master's degree in applied behavior science from The Johns Hopkins University.

GLOSSARY

Cause analysis: The process of determining the root cause(s) of past, present, or future performance gaps. It follows, but is integrally related to, performance analysis.

Competencies: "Internal capabilities that people bring to their jobs. They may be expressed in a broad, even infinite, array of on-the-job behaviors." (McLagan, 1989, p. 77). The skills and knowledge people need to successfully do their jobs.

Enabling output: A specific output associated with the demonstration of a particular competency.

Front-end analysis: Synonymous with performance analysis.

Human performance improvement: The systematic process of discovering and analyzing important human performance gaps, planning for future improvements in human performance, designing and developing cost-effective and ethically justifiable interventions to close performance gaps, implementing the interventions, and evaluating the financial and nonfinancial results.

Human performance improvement process model: A six-step model that describes key steps in conducting human performance improvement work.

Human performance technology: "The total performance improvement system is a merger of systematic performance analysis with comprehensive human resource interventions. And the science of linking the total system together is known as human performance technology." (Rosenberg, 1990, p. 46).

Intervention: A long-term, evolutionary and progressive change effort.

Output: "A product or service that an individual or group delivers to others, especially to colleagues, customers, or clients." (McLagan, 1989, p. 77). See *enabling output* and *terminal output*.

Performance analysis: The process of identifying the organization's performance requirements and comparing them to its objectives and capabilities.

Role: A part played by a person involved in human performance improvement work.

Terminal output: A final outcome directly associated with a particular role.

REFERENCES

Preface

Dixon, N., and Henkelman, J. (1991). *Models for HRD practice: The academic guide*. Alexandria, VA: The American Society for Training and Development.

McLagan, P. (1989). *Models for HRD practice*. Alexandria, VA: The American Society for Training and Development.

McLagan, P., and McCullough, R. (1983). *Models for excellence: The conclusions and recommendations of the ASTD training and development competency study*. Alexandria, VA: The American Society for Training and Development.

Pinto, P., and Walker, J. (1978). *A study of professional training and development roles and competencies*. Madison, WI: The American Society for Training and Development.

Section 1

Bengtson, B. (1994). An analysis of CEO perceptions concerning trainer roles in selected Central Pennsylvania manufacturing firms. Unpublished doctoral dissertation, Pennsylvania State University.

Cameron, W. (1988). *Training competencies of human resource development specialists in Tennessee*. Summary Report, Research Series No. 1. Knoxville, TN: University of Tennessee.

Carr, C. (1992). How performance happens (and how to help it happen better), Part 12: Ten keys to successful performance facilitation. *Performance & Instruction, 31*(1), 36-40.

Davidove, E. (1991). The most important lesson I've learned as a consultant about the systems approach to instructional design. *Performance & Instruction, 31*(10), 11-13.

Dent, J., and Anderson, P. (1998). Fundamentals of HPI. *Info-line*, No. 9811.

de Rijk, R., Mulder, M., and Nijhof, W. (1994). Role profiles of HRD practitioners in 4 European countries. Paper presented at conference, Education for Work. University of Milan, Milan, Italy. Twente: University of Twente.

Dixon, V., Conway, K., Ashley, K., and Stewart, N. (1995). *Training competency architecture toolkit*. Toronto: Ontario Society for Training and Development.

Dixon, V., Conway, K., Ashley, K., and Stewart, N. (1995).*Training competency architecture toolkit*. Toronto: Ontario Society for Training and Development.

Duncan, J.B., and Powers, E.S. (1992). The politics of intervening in organizations. In H.D. Stolovitch and E.J. Keeps (Eds.), *Handbook of human performance technology: A comprehensive guide for analyzing and solving performance problems in organizations* (pp. 77-93). San Francisco: Jossey-Bass.

Eaves, T. (1985). *Trainer competencies: An examination of existing research*. Milwaukee, WI: National Adult Education Conference of the American Association for Adult and Continuing Education.

Foshay, W., Silber, K., and Westgaard, O. (1986). *Instructional design competencies: The standards*. Iowa City, IA: The International Board of Standards for Training, Performance, and Instruction.

Foshay, W., Silber, K., and Westgaard, O. (1988). *Instructors competencies: Volume 1: The standards*. Iowa City, IA: The International Board of Standards for Training, Performance, and Instruction.

Foshay, W., Silber, K., and Westgaard, O., (1990). *Training manager competencies: The standards*. Iowa City, IA: The International Board of Standards for Training, Performance, and Instruction.

Gayeski, D. (1993). Re-framing the practice of training, PT, and corporate communication—Part 4: Reduce (not just produce) information. *Performance & Instruction, 32*(10), 37-40.

Geis, G.L., and Smith, M.E. (1992). The function of evaluation. In H.D. Stolovitch and E.J. Keeps (Eds.), *Handbook of human performance technology: A comprehensive guide for analyzing and solving performance problems in organizations* (pp. 130-150). San Francisco: Jossey-Bass.

Gilbert, T. (1992). Foreword. In H.D. Stolovitch and E.J. Keeps (Eds.), *Handbook of human performance technology: A comprehensive guide for analyzing and solving performance problems in organizations* (pp. xiii-xviii). San Francisco: Jossey-Bass.

Ginkel, K., Mulder, M., and Nijhof, W. (1994). Role profiles of HRD professionals in the Netherlands. Paper presented at conference, Education and Training for Work. University of Milan, Milan, Italy. Twente: University of Twente.

Hutchison, C. (1990). What's a nice P. T. like you doing? *Performance & Instruction, 29*(9), 1-5.

Hutchison, C., Kirkhorn, J., Shmikler, S., Newell, K., and Wills, J. (1988). Leadership skills. *Performance & Instruction, 27*(8), 2-5.

Jewell, S.F., and Jewell, D.O. (1992). Organization design. In H.D. Stolovitch and E.J. Keeps (Eds.), *Handbook of human performance technology: A comprehensive guide for analyzing and solving performance problems in organizations* (pp. 211-232). San Francisco: Jossey-Bass.

Lawson, T. (1990). *The competency initiative: Standards of excellence for human resource executives.* Minneapolis, MN: Golle & Holmes Custom Education.

Lee, S. (1994). A preliminary study of the competencies, work outputs, and roles of human resource development professionals in the Republic of China on Taiwan: A cross-cultural competency study. Unpublished doctoral dissertation, Pennsylvania State University.

Lippitt, G., and Nadler, L. (1967). Emerging roles of the training director. *Training & Development Journal, 21*(8), 2-10.

McLagan, P. (1989). *Models for HRD Practice.* Alexandria, VA: The American Society for Training and Development.

McLagan, P., and McCullough, R. (1983). *Models for excellence: The conclusions and recommendations of the ASTD training and development competency study.* Alexandria, VA: The American Society for Training and Development.

McLean, G., and Sullivan, R. (1995). Essential competencies of internal and external OD consultants. In W. Rothwell, R. Sullivan, and G. McLean (Eds.), *Practicing organization development: A handbook for consultants.* San Diego: Pfeiffer & Co.

Marquardt, M., and Engel, D. (1993). *Global human resource development.* Englewood Cliffs, NJ: Prentice-Hall.

National standards for training and development. (1992). England: Training & Development Lead Body.

Toronto: Ontario Society for Training and Development. (1976). *Core competencies for training and development.*

Patterson, A. (1985). Preparing educational technologists. *Training & Development Journal, 39*(12), 38-39.

Pinto, P., and Walker, J. (1978). *A study of professional training and development roles and competencies.* Madison, WI: The American Society for Training and Development.

Pipe, P. (1992). Ergonomic performance aids. In H.D. Stolovitch and E.J. Keeps (Eds.), *Handbook of human performance technology: A comprehensive guide for analyzing and solving performance problems in organizations* (pp. 352-364). San Francisco: Jossey-Bass.

Ray, J., and Sword, S. (1993). Emerging Technologies—Part 4. Reengineering and human performance. *Performance & Instruction, 32*(7), 29-35.

Rothwell, W., and Kazanas, H. (1994). *Human resource development: A strategic approach.* (Rev. ed.). Amherst, MA: HRD Press.

Rothwell, W., and Kazanas, H. (1992). *Mastering the instructional design process: A systematic approach.* San Francisco: Jossey-Bass.

Rummler, G.A., and Brache, A.P. (1992). Transforming organizations through human performance technology. In H.D. Stolovitch and E.J. Keeps (Eds.), *Handbook of human performance technology: A comprehensive guide for analyzing and solving performance problems in organizations* (pp. 32-49). San Francisco: Jossey-Bass.

The Secretary's Commission on Achieving Necessary Skills. (1991). *Skills and tasks for jobs: A SCANS report for America 2000.* Washington, DC: United States Department of Labor.

Sink, D.L. (1992). Success strategies for the human performance technologist. In H.D. Stolovitch and E.J. Keeps (Eds.), *Handbook of human performance technology: A comprehensive guide for analyzing and solving performance problems in organizations* (pp. 564-575). San Francisco: Jossey-Bass.

Spitzer, D.R. (1992). The design and development of effective interventions. In H.D. Stolovitch and E.J. Keeps (Eds.), *Handbook of human performance technology: A comprehensive guide for analyzing and solving performance problems in organizations* (pp. 114-129). San Francisco: Jossey-Bass.

Spitzer, D. (1988). Instructional/performance technology competencies. *Performance & Instruction, 27*(7), 11-13.

Steininger, T. (1990). Leaders—the good, the bad and the ugly. *Performance & Instruction, 29*(7), 3.

Stolovitch, H.D., Keeps, E.J., and Rodrigue, D. (1995). Skills sets for the human performance technologist. *Performance Improvement Quarterly, 8*(2), 40-67.

Tosti, D., and Jackson, S. (1992). Influencing others to act. In H.D. Stolovitch and E.J. Keeps (Eds.), *Handbook of human performance technology: A comprehensive guide for analyzing and solving performance problems in organizations* (pp. 551-563). San Francisco: Jossey-Bass.

U.S. Civil Service Commission. (1976). *The employee development specialist curriculum plan: An outline of learning experiences for the employee development specialist.*

Westgaard, O. (1992). Standards and ethics for practitioners. In H.D. Stolovitch and E.J. Keeps (Eds.), *Handbook of human performance technology: A comprehensive guide for analyzing and solving performance problems in organizations* (pp. 576-585). San Francisco: Jossey-Bass.

Workplace trainer competency standards. (1994). Australia: Competency Standards Body—Assessors & Workplace Trainers.

Zigon, J. (1987). Marketing, not selling, performance technology to top management. *Performance & Instruction, 26*(7), 9-15.

Section 2

Anonymous. 1995 Industry Report. *Training 32*(10), 37-74.

Coleman, M.E. (1992). Developing skills and enhancing professional competence. In H.D. Stolovitch and E.J. Keeps (Eds.), *Handbook of human performance technology: A comprehensive guide for analyzing and solving performance problems in organizations* (pp. 634-647). San Francisco: Jossey-Bass.

Deterline, W.A., and Rosenberg, M.J. (Eds.). (1992). *Workplace productivity: Performance technology success stories.* Washington, DC: ISPI.

Dixon, G. (Ed.). (1988). *What works at work: Lessons from the masters.* Minneapolis: Lakewood Publications.

Dormant, D. (1992). Implementing human performance technology in organizations. In H.D. Stolovitch and E.J. Keeps (Eds.), *Handbook of human performance technology: A comprehensive guide for analyzing and solving performance problems in organizations* (pp. 167-187). San Francisco: Jossey-Bass.

Geis, G.L. (1986). Human performance technology: An overview. In M. E. Smith (Ed.), *Introduction to performance technology* (pp. 1-20). Washington, DC: National Society for Performance and Instruction.

Gilbert, T.F. (1978). *Human competence: Engineering worthy performance.* New York: McGraw-Hill.

Harless, J. H. (1986). Guiding performance with job aids. In M.E. Smith (Ed.), *Introduction to performance technology* (pp. 106-124). Washington, DC: National Society for Performance and Instruction.

Hutchison, C. S. (1990). A performance technology process model. *Performance & Instruction, 29*(3), 1-5.

Kirkpatrick, D.L. (Ed.). (1975). *Evaluating training programs.* Alexandria, VA: American Society for Training and Development.

Lyau, N. and Pucel, D. (1995). Economic return on training investment at the organizational level. *Performance Improvement Quarterly, 8*(3), 68-79.

Mager, R.F. (1988). *Making instruction work or skillblockers.* Belmont, CA: David S. Lake.

Ray, J.S. (1993). Emerging technologies—Part 4: Reengineering and human performance. *Performance & Instruction, 32*(7), 29-35.

Rosenberg, M.J., Coscarelli, W.C., and Hutchison, D.S. (1992). The origins and evolution of the field. In H.D. Stolovitch & E.J. Keeps (Eds.), *Handbook of human performance technology: A comprehensive guide for analyzing and solving performance problems in organizations* (pp. 14-31). San Francisco: Jossey-Bass.

Rosenberg, M.J. (1990). Performance technology: Working the system. *Training, 27*(2), 43-48.

Rosenberg, M.J. (1982). Our instructional media roots. *Performance & Instruction, 21*(3).

Rossett, A. (1992). Analysis of human performance problems. In H.D. Stolovitch and E.J. Keeps (Eds.), *Handbook of human performance technology: A comprehensive guide for analyzing and solving performance problems in organizations* (pp. 97-113). San Francisco: Jossey-Bass.

Rossett, A. (1987). *Training needs assessment: Techniques in training and performance.* Englewood Cliffs, NJ: Educational Technology Publications.

Rummler, G.A., and Brache, A.P. (1992). Transforming organizations through human performance technology. In H.D. Stolovitch and E.J. Keeps (Eds.), *Handbook of human performance technology: A comprehensive guide for analyzing and solving performance problems in organizations* (pp. 32-49). San Francisco: Jossey-Bass, 1992.

Rummler, G.A., and Brache, A.P. (1988). The systems view of human performance. *Training, 25*(9), 45-53.

Rummler, G.A. (1986). Organizational redesign. In M.E. Smith (Ed.), *Introduction to performance technology* (pp. 211-235). Washington, DC: National Society for Performance and Instruction.

Senge, P. (1990). *The fifth discipline: The art and practice of the learning organization.* New York: Doubleday.

Sharpe, C. (Ed.). (1998). *The Info-line Guide to Performance Improvement.* Alexandria, VA: ASTD.

Spitzer, D.R. (1992). The design and development of effective interventions. In H.D. Stolovitch and E.J. Keeps (Eds.), *Handbook of human performance technology: A comprehensive guide for analyzing and solving performance problems in organizations* (pp. 114-129). San Francisco: Jossey-Bass.

Stolovitch, H.D., Keeps, E.J., and Rodrigue, D. (1995). Skill sets for the human performance technologist. *Performance Improvement Quarterly, 8*(2), 40-67.

Section 3

1995 American Management Association survey. New York: American Management Association.

1995 Computer-based training report: A comprehensive study of CBT and the future of multimedia as an instructional delivery system. Patricia Seybold Group.

Farber, H.S. The changing face of job loss in the United States, 1982-1993. Unpublished manuscript.

Hamermesh, D.S., and Rees, A. (1992). *The economics of work and pay.* (5th ed.). New York: Harper College Publishers.

Hornbeck, D.W., and Salamon, L.M. (Eds.). (1991). *Human capital and America's future: An economic strategy for the '90s.* Baltimore: Johns Hopkins University Press.

Ichniowski, C., Shaw, K., and Prennushi, G. (1996). *The effects of human resource management practices on productivity.* Unpublished manuscript. New York: Columbia University.

Johnston, W.B., and Packer, A.H. (Eds.). (1987). *Workforce 2000: Work and workers for the twenty-first century.* Indianapolis, IN: Hudson Institute.

Lawler III, E., Mohrman, S.A., and Ledford Jr., G.E. (Eds.). (1995). *Creating high performance organizations: Practices and results of employee involvement and total quality management in Fortune 1000 companies.* San Francisco: Jossey-Bass.

President. (1996). *Economic report of the President.* Washington, DC: U.S. Government Printing Office.

Survey of American business leaders. (1995). Deloitte & Touche.

Technology in the training department: Impact and implications. (1995). Lakewood Research.

U.S. Department of Labor. (1995). *Report on the American workforce.*

U.S. Department of Labor. (1994). *Report on the American workforce.*

Section 4

Brinkerhoff, R.O. (1994). *The learning alliance: Systems thinking in human resource development.* San Francisco: Jossey-Bass.

Dean, P.J. (Ed.). (1994). *Performance engineering at work.* Batavia, Illinois: International Board of Standards for Training, Performance, and Instruction.

Dent, J., and Anderson, P. (1998).The Fundamentals of HPI. *Info-line,* No. 9811.

Gery, G.J. (1991). *Electronic performance support systems.* Boston: Weingarten.

Gilbert, T.F. (1978). *Human competence: Engineering worthy performance.* New York: McGraw-Hill.

Gilbert, T.F. (1982a). A question of performance—Part I: The PROBE model. *Training & Development Journal,* 36(9), 20-30.

Gilbert, T.F. (1982b). A question of performance—Part II: Applying the PROBE model. *Training & Development Journal,* 36(10), 85-89.

Langdon, D.G. (1995). *The new language of work.* Amherst, MA: HRD Press.

Mager, R.F., and Pipe, P. (1984). *Analyzing performance problems, or you really oughta wanna.* (2d ed.). Belmont, CA: David S. Lake.

Performance Improvement Quarterly. (1995). Special Issue on Electronic Performance Support Systems, 8(1).

Performance Improvement Quarterly. (1995). Special Issue on the Changing Roles of Human Performance Technology, 8(2).

Performance Improvement Quarterly. (1995). Special Issue on Performance Technologist Preparation: Investing in Our Future, 8(4).

Robinson, D.G., and Robinson, J.C. (1995). *Performance consulting: Moving beyond training.* San Francisco: Berrett-Koehler.

Rosenberg, M.J. (1989). Performance technology working the system. *Performance Technology,* 5, 5-10.

Rummler, G.A., and Brache, A.P. (1990). *Improving performance: How to manage the white space on the organization chart.* San Francisco: Jossey-Bass.

Stolovitch, H.D., and Keeps, E.J. (Eds.). (1992). *Handbook of human performance technology: A comprehensive guide for analyzing and solving performance problems in organizations.* San Francisco: Jossey-Bass.

Swanson, R.A. (1994). *Analysis for improving performance: Tools for diagnosing organizations and documenting workplace expertise.* San Francisco: Berrett-Koehler.

Winslow, C.D., and Bramer, W.L. (1994). *FutureWork: Putting knowledge to work in the knowledge economy.* New York: The Free Press.

Section 5

Callahan, M. (1998). The Role of the Performance Evaluator. *Info-line,* No. 9803

_____ . (1997). The Role of the Performance Intervention Specialist. *Info-line,* No. 9714.

Kirrane, D. (1997). The Role of the Performance Needs Analyst. *Info-line,* No. 9713.

Koehle, D. (1997). The Role of the Performance Change Manager. *Info-line,* No. 9715.

McLagan, P. (1989). *Models for HRD practice.* Alexandria, VA: The American Society for Training and Development.

Rothwell, W. (1996). *Beyond training and development: State-of-the-art strategies for enhancing human performance.* New York: AMACOM.

Stolovitch, H.D., and Keeps, E.J. (Eds.). (1992). *Handbook of human performance technology: A comprehensive guide for analyzing and solving performance problems in organizations.* San Francisco: Jossey-Bass.

Section 6

Arthur Andersen & Co. (1992). *Ethics for managers: Instructors guide.* St. Charles, IL.

Andrews, K.R. (1989). Ethics in practice. *Harvard Business Review,* 67(5), 99-104.

Aresty Institute of Executive Education (1988). *Business ethics study guide*. Philadelphia, PA: University of Pennsylvania, Wharton School of Business.

Baron, D. (1991). *Business and its environment*. Englewood Cliffs, NJ: Prentice-Hall.

Beauchamp, T.L., and Bowie, N.E. (Eds.). (1988). *Ethical theory and business*. (3d ed.). Englewood Cliffs, NJ: Prentice Hall.

Bednar, A.K. (1988). Needs assessment as a change strategy: A case study. *Performance Improvement Quarterly*, *1*(2), 31-39.

Bennis, W.G., and Slater, P.E. (1968). *The temporary society*. New York: Harper & Row.

Bentham, J. (1970). *An introduction to the principle of morals and legislation*. London: Athlone Press.

Berenbeim, R.E. (1987). *Corporate ethics* (Research Report #900). New York: The Conference Board.

Beyer, J.M., and Trice, H.M. (1987). How an organization's rites reveal its culture. *Organizational Dynamics*, *15*(4), 4-24.

Bok, S. (1980). Whistleblowing and professional responsibilities. In D. Callahan and S. Bok (Eds.), *Ethics teaching in higher education*. New York, NY: Plenum.

Bommer, M., Gratto, C., Gravander, J., and Tuttle, M. (1987). A behavioral model of ethical and unethical decision making. *Journal of Business Ethics*, *6*(4), 265-280.

Brady, F.N. (1990). *Ethical managing: Rules and results*. New York: Macmillan.

Cavanagh, G.F., Moberg, D.J., and Velasquez, M. (1981). The ethics of organizational politics. *Academy of Management Review*, *66*, 363-374.

Colby, A., et al. (1983). A longitudinal study of moral judgement. *Monographs of the Society for Research in Child Development*, *48*(1-2), 1-124.

Cooke, R.A. (1992). *Ethics in business: A perspective*. Business Ethics Program. St. Charles, IL: Arthur Andersen & Co.

CPCU Society/American Institute for Property and Liability Underwriters (1991). *Guidelines for ethical decision making*. Malvern, PA.

Daniels, N. (1978). Merit and meritocracy. *Philosophy & Public Affairs*, *7*, 206-223.

Deal, T.E., and Kennedy, A.A. (1982). *Corporate cultures: The rites and rituals of corporate life*. Reading, MA: Addison-Wesley.

Dean, P.J. (1992a). Making codes of ethics 'real.' *Journal of Business Ethics*, *11*(4), 285-290.

Dean, P.J. (1992b). Allow me to introduce...Tom Gilbert. *Performance Improvement Quarterly*, *5*(3), 83-95.

Dean, P.J. (1993). A selected review of the underpinnings of ethics for human performance technology professionals, Parts 1 and 2. *Performance Improvement Quarterly*, *6*(4), 3-49.

Dean, P.J. (1994). Customizing codes of ethics to set professional standards. *Performance & Instruction*, *32*(2), 36-45.

DeGeorge, R.T. (1987). The status of business ethics: past and future. *Journal of Business Ethics*, *6*(3), 201-211.

Derry, R., (1987). Moral reasoning in work-related conflicts. In W.C. Frederick and L.E. Preston (Eds.), *Research in corporate and social performance and policy* (pp. 25-49). Greenwich, CT: JAI Press.

Derry, R. and Green, R.M. (1989). Ethical theory in business ethics: a critical assessment. *Journal of Business Ethics*, *8*(7), 521-533.

Dubinsky, A.J., and Loken, B. (1989). Analyzing ethical decision making in marketing. *Journal of Business Research*, *19*(2), 83-107.

Eells, R. (1962). *The government of corporations*. New York: The Free Press.

Evan, W.M. (1975). Power, conflict and constitutionism in organizations. *Social Science Information*, *14*, 53-80.

Ewing, D.W. (1977). *Freedom inside the organization: Bringing civil liberties to the workplace*. New York: McGraw-Hill.

Ewing, D.W. (1981). Constitutionalizing the corporation. In T. Bradshaw and D. Vogel (Eds.), *Corporations and their culture*. New York: McGraw-Hill.

Feinberg, J. (1973). *Social philosophy*. Englewood Cliffs, NJ: Prentice-Hall.

Ferrell, O.C., and Gresham, L.G. (1985). A contingency framework for understanding ethical decision making in marketing. *Journal of Marketing, 49*(Spring), 87-96.

Ferrell, O.C., and Fraedrich, J. (1991). *Business ethics: Ethical decision making and cases*. Boston, MA: Houghton Mifflin.

Fleming, J. (1987). A survey and critique of business ethics research. In W. Frederick (Ed.), *Research on corporate social performance and policy* (pp. 1-24). Greenwich, CT: JAI Press.

Freeman, R.E. (Ed.). (1991). *Business ethics: The state of the art*. New York: Oxford University Press.

Fuller, L. (1964). *The morality of law*. New Haven, CT: Yale University Press.

Gilbert, T.F. (1978). *Human competence: Engineering worthy performance*. New York: McGraw-Hill.

Gilligan, C. (1977). In a different voice: Women's conception of the self and morality. *Harvard Educational Review, 49*, 431-446.

Gilligan, C., and Attanucci, J. (1988). Two moral orientations: Gender differences and similarities. *Merril-Palmer Quarterly, 34*(3), 223-237.

Glazer, M.P., and Glazer, P.M. (1989). Whistleblowing. *Psychology Today, 20*(8), 37-43.

Gustafson, J.M. (1991). Ethics: An American growth industry. *The Key Reporter, 56*(3).

Hammond, J.D. (1992). Internal communication, Penn State University Smeal College of Business.

Harless, J.H. (1973). An analysis of front-end analysis. *Improving Human Performance, 4*, 229-244.

Hart, H.L.A. (1955). Are there any natural rights? *Philosophical Press, 64*, 175-191.

Hegarty, W.H., and Sims, H.P. (1978). Some determinants of unethical decision behavior: An experiment. *Journal of Applied Psychology, 63*(4), 451-457.

Hegarty, W.H., and Sims, H.P. (1979). Organizational philosophy, policies, and objectives related to unethical decision behavior: A laboratory experiment. *Journal of Applied Psychology, 64*(3), 331-338.

Hobbes, T. (1958). *The leviathan*. New York: Macmillan.

Hunt, S.D., and Vitell, S. (1986). A general theory of marketing ethics. *Journal of Macromarketing, 6*(1), 5-16.

Jones, T.M. (1991). Ethical decision making by individuals in organizations: An issue-contingent model. *Academy of Management Review, 16*(2), 366-395.

Kahn, W.A. (1990). Toward an agenda for business ethics research. *Academy of Management Review, 15*(2), 311-328.

Kamm, J.B. (1991). Personal correspondence.

Kant, I. (1965). *The metaphysical elements of justice*. (J. Ladd, trans). New York: Macmillan.

Kaufman, R. (1986). Obtaining functional results: Relating needs assessment, needs analysis, and objectives. *Educational Technology, 26*(1), 24-27.

Keeley, M. (1979). *Justice versus effectiveness in organizational evaluation*. Paper presented at the annual meeting of the Academy of Management, Atlanta.

Kohlberg, L. (1969). Stage and sequence: The cognitive-developmental approach to socialization. In D.A. Goslin (Ed.), *Handbook of socialization* (pp. 347-480). Chicago: Rand-McNally.

Krupp, S. (1961). *Pattern in organizational analysis: A critical examination*. New York: Holt, Rinehart & Winston.

Kurtines, Azmitia, and Alvarez (1990). Science and morality: The role of values in science and the scientific study of moral phenomena. *Psychological Bulletin, 107*(3), 283-295.

Locke, J. (1952). *The second treatise of government*. New York: Liberal Arts Press.

McLagan, P. (1983). The concept of responsibility: Some implications for organizational behavior and development. *Journal of Management Studies, 20*(4), 411-423.

Mager, R.F., and Pipe, P. (1984). *Analyzing performance problems or you really oughta wanna*. (2d ed.). Belmont, CA: David S. Lake.

Martin, J., and Siehl, C. (1983). Organizational culture and counterculture: An uneasy symbiosis. *Organizational Dynamics*, Autumn, 12(2), 52-64.

Milgram, S. (1974). *Obedience to authority: An experimental view*. New York: Harper & Row.

Mill, J.S. (1957). *Utilitarianism*. Indianapolis, IN: Bobbs-Merrill.

Miller, A.R. (1971). *The assault on privacy: Computers, databanks, and dossiers*. Ann Arbor, MI: University of Michigan Press.

Mironi, M. (1974). The confidentiality of personal records: A legal and ethical view. *Labor Law Journal, 25*, 270-292.

Murphy, P.E. (1989). Creating ethical corporate structures. *Sloan Management Review*, Winter, 30(2), 81-87.

Navran, F. (1990). *Ethics effectiveness quick-test*. Atlanta, GA: Navran Associates.

Perry, D., Bennet, K., and Edwards, G. (1990). *Ethics policies and programs*. Washington, DC: Ethics Resource Center.

Pfeffer, J. (1978). The micropolitics of organizations. In M.W. Meyer et al. (Eds.), *Environments and organizations* (pp. 29-50). San Francisco, CA: Jossey-Bass.

Piaget, J. (1932). *The moral judgement of the child*. London: K. Paul, Trench, Trubner & Company.

Pojman, L.P. (Ed.). (1989). *Ethical theory: Classical and contemporary readings*. Belmont, CA: Wadsworth.

Rawls, J. (1971). *A theory of justice*. Cambridge, MA: Belknap Press.

Rest, J.R. (1986). *Moral development: Advances in research and theory*. New York: Praeger.

Robin, D., Giallourakis, M., David, F.R., and Moritz, T.E. (1989). A different look at codes of ethics. *Business Horizons, 32*(1), 66-73.

Rossett, A. (1987). *Training needs assessment: Techniques in training and performance development*. Englewood Cliffs, NJ: Educational Technology Publications.

Rummler, G.A., and Brache, A.P. (1990). *Improving performance: How to manage the white space on the organization chart*. San Francisco, CA: Jossey-Bass.

Schein, E.H. (1985). How culture forms, develops, and changes. In R.H. Kilmann, M.J. Saxton, and R. Serpa (Eds.), *Gaining control of the corporate culture* (pp. 17-43). San Francisco, CA: Jossey-Bass.

Schwartz, H., and Davis, S.M. (1981). Matching corporate culture and business strategy. *Organizational Dynamics*, Summer, 10(1), 30-48.

Sharpe, C. (Ed.). (1998). *The Info-line Guide to Performance Improvement*. Alexandria, VA: ASTD

Shaw, W., and Barry, V. (1989). *Moral issues in business*. (4th ed.). Belmont, CA: Wadsworth.

Sidgwick, H. (1966). *The methods of ethics*. New York: Dover.

Smith, A. (1759). *Essays philosophical and literary*. London: Ward, Lock, & Co.

Smith, A. (1937). *An inquiry into the nature and causes of the wealth of nations*. New York: The Modern Library.

Stolovitch, H.D., and Keeps, E.J. (Eds.). (1992). *Handbook of human performance technology: A comprehensive guide for analyzing and solving performance problems in organizations*. San Francisco: Jossey-Bass.

Sturdivant, F.D., and Wortzel, H.V. (1990). *Business and society: A managerial approach*. (4th ed.). Homewood, IL: Irwin.

Trevino, L.K., Sutton, C.D., and Woodman, R.W. (1985, August). Effects of reinforcement contingencies and cognitive moral development on ethical decision-making behavior: An experiment. Paper presented at the annual meeting of the Academy of Management, San Diego.

Trevino, L.K. (1986). Ethical decision making in organizations: A person-situation interactionist model. *Academy of Management Review, 11*(3), 601-617.

Trevino, L.K. (1987). The influences of vicarious learning and individual differences on ethical decision making in the organization: An experiment. Unpublished doctoral dissertation, Texas A&M University.

Trevino, L.K. (1990). A cultural perspective on changing and developing organizational ethics. In R.W. Woodman and W. Passmore (Eds.), *Research in Organizational Change and Development, 4*, 194-230.

Trevino, L.K., and Weaver, G.R. (1991). Business ETHICS/BUSINESS ethics: One field or two? Paper presented at the annual meeting of the Academy of Management, Miami, FL.

Trevino, L.K. (1992). Moral reasoning and business ethics: Implications for research, education and management. *Journal of Business Ethics, 11*(5-6), 445-459.

Turiel, E. (1969). Developmental processes in the child's moral thinking. In P.H. Mussen, J. Langer, and M. Covington (Eds.), *Trends and issues in developmental psychology*. New York: Holt, Rinehart & Winston.

Velasquez, M.G., Cavanagh, G., and Moberg, D. (1983). Organizational statesmanship and dirty politics: Ethical guidelines for the organizational politician. *Organizational Dynamics*, Autumn, 12(2).

Velasquez, M.G. (1992). *Business ethics: Concepts and cases*. (3d ed.). Englewood Cliffs, NJ: Prentice-Hall.

Wagner, M.F. (1991). *An historical introduction to moral philosophy*. Englewood Cliffs, NJ: Prentice-Hall.

Walters, K.D. (1975). Your employee's right to blow the whistle. *Harvard Business Review, 53*(4), 26-34.

Waltzer, M. (1967). The obligation to disobey. *Ethics, 77*(3), 163-175.

Wasserstrom, R. (1978). Privacy and the law. In R. Bronaugh (Ed.), *Philosophical law: Authority, equality, adjudication, privacy*. Westport, CT: Greenwood Press.

Weber, J. (1990). Manager's moral reasoning: Assessing their responses to three moral dilemmas. *Human Relations, 43*, 687-702.

Werhane, P.H. (1992, July). Business Ethics Program. St. Charles, IL: Arthur Andersen & Co. Corporate moral and social responsibility. Paper presented at Ethics Practice and Teaching Workshop, Colorado Springs, CO.

Westgaard, O. (1988). *A credo for performance technologists*. Western Springs, IL: International Board of Standards for Training, Performance, and Instruction.

Performance Improvement References

Argyris, C. (1964). *Integrating the individual and the organization*. New York: Wiley.

Argyris, C., and Schon, D. A. (1978). *Organizational learning: A theory of action perspective*. Reading, MA: Addison-Wesley.

Argyris, C. (1990). *Overcoming organizational defenses: Facilitating organizational learning*. Needlam, MA: Allyn and Bacon.

Bandura, A. (1977). *Social learning theory*. Englewood Cliffs, NJ: Prentice-Hall.

Block, P. (1981). *Flawless consulting learning concepts: A guide to getting your expertise used*. Austin, TX.

Block, P. (1993). *Stewardship: Choosing service over self-interest*. San Francisco, CA: Berrett-Koehler.

Burke, W. W. (1982). *Organization development: principles and practices*. Boston: Little, Brown.

Carkhuff, R. R. (1984). *The exemplar: The exemplary performer in the age of productivity*. Amherst, MA: HRD Press.

Carkhuff, R. R. (1986). *Human processing and human productivity*. Amherst, MA: HRD Press.

Cartwright, D. (Ed.). (1951). *Field theory in social science: Selected theoretical papers*. New York: Harper-Collins.

Dean, P.J. (1994). *Performance engineering at work*. Batavia, IL: International Board of Standards for Training, Performance, and Instruction.

Flanagan, J.C. (1954). The critical incident technique. *Psychological Bulletin, 51*, 327-343.

Gery, G. (1991). *Electronic performance support systems: How and why to remake the workplace through the strategic application of technology.* Boston: Weingarten Publications.

Gilbert, T.F. (1962). Mathetics: The technology of education. *The Journal of Mathetics, January,* 7-73.

Gilbert, T.F. (1976). Saying what a subject matter is. *Instructional Science, 5,* 29-53.

Gilbert, T.F. (1978). *Human competence: Engineering worthy performance.* New York: McGraw-Hill.

Gilbert, T. (1978). Guiding worthy performance. *Improving Human Performance Quarterly, 7*(3), 273-302.

Gilbert, T. F. (1982). A question of performance—Part I: The PROBE model. *Training & Development Journal, 36*(9), 21-30.

Gilbert, T.F. (1982). A question of performance—Part II: Applying the PROBE model. *Training & Development Journal, 36*(10), 85-89.

Gilbert, T.F. (1987). Measuring performance at work. In D. Fishman and D. Peterson (Eds.), *Assessment for decision* (pp. 355-389). New Brunswick, NJ: Rutgers University Press.

Gilbert, T.F. (1988). Measuring the potential for performance improvement. *Training, 25*(7), 49-55.

Gilbert, T.F., and Gilbert, M.B. (1988). The science of winning. *Training, 25*(8), 34-40.

Gilbert, T.F., and Gilbert M.B. (1989). Performance engineering: Making human productivity a science. *Performance & Instruction, 28*(1), 3-9.

Harless, J. (1970). *An ounce of analysis (is worth a pound of objectives).* Newnan, GA: Harless Performance Guild.

Harless, J. (1973). An analysis of front-end analysis. *Improving Human Performance, 4.*

IBSTPI (International Board of Standards for Training, Performance & Instruction) Publications. Barrington, IL.
   Instructional design competencies: The standards. (1994).

   Instructor competencies: The standards: Volume 1. (1993).
   Instructor competencies: The standards: Volume 2. (1993).
   Training manager competencies: The standards. (1994).

Jaques, E., (1976). *A general theory of bureaucracy.* London: Heinemann.

Jaques, E. and Clement, S. D. (1994). *Executive leadership: A practical guide to managing complexity.* Arlington, VA: Basil Blackwell.

Kaufman, R. (1986). Obtaining functional results: Relating needs assessment, needs analysis, and objectives. *Educational Technology, 26*(1), 24-26.

Kaufman, R., Thiagarajan, S., and MacGillis, P. (1995). *The practitioner's handbook on organization and human performance improvement.* San Diego: University Associates/Pfeiffer and Company.

Kolb, D.A. (1984). *Experiential learning: Experience as the source of learning and development.* Englewood Cliffs, NJ: Prentice-Hall.

Kotter, J. P. (1978). *Organizational dynamics: Diagnosis and intervention.* Reading, MA: Addison-Wesley.

Kotter J.P., and Heskett, J.L. (1992). *Corporate culture and performance.* New York: The Free Press.

Langdon, D.G. (1973). *Interactive instructional designs for individualized learning.* Englewood Cliffs, NJ: Educational Technology Publications, Inc.

Langdon, D.G. (1995). *The new language of work.* Amherst, MA: HRD Press.

Lepper, M.R., and Greene, D. (1978). *The hidden costs of reward: New perspectives on the psychology of human motivation.* Hillsdale, N.J: Lawrence Erlbaum Associates.

Lewin, G.W. (Ed.). (1948). *Resolving social conflicts: Selected papers on group dynamics.* New York: Harper-Collins.

Likert, R. (1967). *The human organization: Its management and value.* New York: McGraw-Hill.

McGregor, D. (1960). *The human side of enterprise.* New York: McGraw-Hill.

McLagan, P. (1983). *Models for excellence.* Alexandria, VA: American Society for Training and Development.

McLagan, P.A. (1989). *Models for HRD practice.* Alexandria, VA: American Society for Training and Development, Alexandria, VA.

Mager, R.F., and Pipe, P. (1970). *Analyzing performance problems or you really oughta wanna.* (2d ed.). Belmont, CA: David S. Lake.

Mager, R.F. (1984). *Goal analysis.* Belmont, CA: David S. Lake.

Mager, R.F. (1984). *Making instruction work.* Belmont, CA: David S. Lake.

Mager, R.F. (1984). *Measuring instructional results.* Belmont, CA: David S. Lake.

Mager, R.F. (1984). *Preparing instructional objectives.* Belmont, CA: David S. Lake.

Mager, R.F. (1984). *Developing attitude toward learning.* Belmont, CA: David S. Lake.

Mintzberg, H. (1976). Planning on the left side and managing on the right. *Harvard Business Review, 54* (4), pp. 49-58.

Nisbett, R., and Ross, L. (1980). *Human inference: Strategies and shortcomings of social judgment.* Englewood, Cliffs, NJ: Prentice-Hall.

Odiorne, G.S. (1987). *The human side of management: Management by integration and self-control.* San Diego: Lexington Books and University Associates.

Reigeluth, C.M. (1983) *Instructional-design theories and models: An overview of their current status.* Hillsdale, NJ: Lawrence Erlbaum Associates.

Renier, J.J. (1986). Ethical infrastructure: Vital to productivity gains. *World of Work Report, 11*(1), 4-5.

Revans, R.W. (1982). *The origins and development of action learning.* England: Brookfield Publishing.

Richey, R.C. (1986). *The theoretical and conceptual bases of instructional design.* New York: Nichols.

Robinson, D.G. and Robinson, J.C. (1995). *Performance consulting: Moving beyond training.* San Francisco: Berrett-Koehler.

Rummler, G.A., and Brache, A.P. (1995). *Improving performance: How to manage the white space on the organization chart.* (2d ed.). San Francisco: Jossey-Bass. Sashkin M. (1984). Participative management is an ethical imperative. *Organizational Dynamics,* Spring, 12(4), 4-22.

Schein, E.H. (1985). *Organizational culture and leadership.* San Francisco: Jossey-Bass.

Schein, E.H. (1987). *Process consultation: Lessons for managers and consultants.* (Vol. 2). Reading, MA: Addison-Wesley.

Stolovitch, H.D., and Keeps, E.J. (Eds.). (1992). *The handbook of human performance technology: A comprehensive guide for analyzing and solving performance problems in organizations.* San Francisco: Jossey-Bass.

Swanson, R.A. (1994). *Analysis for improving performance: Tools for diagnosing organizations and documenting workplace expertise.* San Francisco: Berrett-Koehler.

Taylor, F.W. (1915). *The principles of scientific management.* New York: Harper & Row.

Vaill, P.B. (1989). *Managing as a performing art: New ideas for a world of chaotic change.* San Francisco: Jossey-Bass.

Weisbord, M.R. (1987). *Productive workplaces: Organizing and managing for dignity, meaning, and community.* San Francisco: Jossey-Bass.

Section 7

McLagan, P. (1989). *Models for HRD practice.* Alexandria, VA: The American Society for Training and Development.

Rothwell, W. (1996). *Beyond training and development: State-of-the-art strategies for enhancing human performance.* New York: AMACOM.

Section 8

McLagan, P. (1989). *Models for HRD practice.* Alexandria, VA: The American Society for Training and Development.